THE LAUREL POETRY SERIES *is
unique in the growing range of fine,
inexpensive paperbound books. Each
volume contains the works of a
single poet, along with an original
introduction, a chronology of the
poet's career, a bibliography, and
notes on the poetry.*

G. ROBERT STANGE *has taught at
Harvard and Bennington, and is now
Associate Professor of English at
the University of Minnesota. He is
co-author of "Victorian Poetry and
Poetics" with Walter E. Houghton.*

RICHARD WILBUR, *the General Editor,
has won the Pulitzer Prize, the
National Book Award, and the Millay
Prize, all three in 1957 for his book
of poems, "Things of This World."
He has published several other
volumes of poetry, as well as a
translation of Molière's "The
Misanthrope." Mr. Wilbur has held
a Guggenheim and a Prix de Rome
Fellowship, and is a member of the
National Institute of Arts and Letters.
He is now Professor of English at
Wesleyan University, and has taught
at Harvard and Wellesley.*

The Laurel Poetry Series

General Editor, Richard Wilbur

Coleridge

Selected, with an introduction
and notes, by G. Robert Stange

Published by
DELL PUBLISHING CO., INC.
750 Third Avenue
New York 17, N.Y.

Typography by Alvin Eisenman

Cover drawing by Richard Powers

First printing: March, 1959
Second printing: December, 1959
Third printing: November, 1962

Printed in U.S.A.

Introduction

The greatest obstructions to the respect Coleridge's poetry deserves from us are in some ways the accomplishments of the poet himself. His writings in literary criticism, in religious theory and in philosophy are now so warmly admired that they tend to overshadow all but his greatest poems. And as a more serious diversion leading us away from the poetry there is the biographical Coleridge: no matter how unfamiliar we are with details we all have some conception of this beguiling, many-sided figure. Coleridge the drug-addict, the day-dreamer, the lyrical genius transpiring from a fog of German metaphysics, enrages the moralist, incites the psychologist and bemuses the curious reader. The poet, too, had a habit of dramatizing his worst qualities—a procedure that does not help us in approaching his poetry. It was he who created the legend of his indolence, who cast himself in the role of poetic failure, and who still, in his penitential self-depreciation, almost persuades us that his visionary gleam fled very early, not to appear again.

In reading even the simplest of his poems it is well to keep at the edge of vision the Coleridge who is the greatest of English literary critics, and to remember the metaphysician and theologian. The poetry, however, can stand alone; I propose to examine it without making extensive reference to Coleridge's theoretical writings. To try to describe the nature and extent of the body of poetry he left, to try to see what *kind* of poet he was. We might then begin, not with the biographical Coleridge, but with the image of the poet that seems relevant to a reading of his

verse. Such an approach is desirable not only because of
the interesting difficulties raised by his chameleon per-
sonality, but also because a principal theme of Coleridge's
poetry was *himself*. His friend Wordsworth's most ambitious poem was subtitled, the "Growth of a Poet's Mind";
much of Coleridge's work reveals not so much the growth
of his mind as the activity of that mind analyzed with su-
preme acuity.

Let us begin with the physical man. Here is how Coleridge chose to describe himself in 1796:

> As to me, my face, unless when animated by immedi-
> ate eloquence, expresses great sloth, and great, in-
> deed, almost idiotic good-nature. 'Tis a mere carcass
> of a face, fat, flabby, and expressive chiefly of inex-
> pression. Yet I am told that my eyes, eyebrows, and
> forehead are physiognomically good; but of this the
> deponent knoweth not. As to my shape, 't is a good
> shape enough if measured, but my gait is awkward,
> and the walk of the whole man indicates *indolence
> capable of energies*. I am, and ever have been, a great
> reader, and have read almost everything—a library
> cormorant. I am *deep* in all out of the way books,
> whether of the monkish times, or of the puritanical
> era. I have read and digested most of the historical
> writers; but I do not *like* history. Metaphysics and
> poetry and "facts of mind," that is, accounts of all
> the strange phantasms that ever possessed "your phi-
> losophy"; dreamers, from Thoth the Egyptian to Tay-
> lor the English pagan, are my darling studies. In
> short, I seldom read except to amuse myself, and I
> am almost always reading. Of useful knowledge, I
> am a so-so chemist, and I love chemistry. All else is
> *blank*; but will be (please God) an horticulturalist
> and a farmer. I compose very little, and I absolutely
> hate composition, and such is my dislike that even a
> sense of duty is sometimes too weak to overpower it.

I cannot breathe through my nose, so my mouth,
with sensual thick lips, is almost always open. In con-

versation I am impassioned, and oppose what I deem error with an eagerness which is often mistaken for personal asperity; but I am ever so swallowed up in the *thing* that I perfectly forget my *opponent.* Such am I. . . .

And yet in a celebrated description William Hazlitt, who was not given to overlooking the faults of others, records a significantly different impression. He describes his conviction, on hearing Coleridge preach in a Unitarian chapel in 1798, that "Poetry and Philosophy had met together. Truth and Genius had embraced under the eye and with the sanction of Religion." And the appearance of this "half-inspired" speaker was, for Hazlitt, no less impressive:

> His forehead was broad and high, light as if built of ivory, with large projecting eyebrows, and his eyes rolling beneath them, like a sea with darkened lustre. "A certain tender bloom his face o'erspread," a purple tinge as we see it in the pale thoughtful complexions of the Spanish portrait-painters, Murillo and Velasquez. His mouth was gross, voluptuous, open, eloquent; his chin good-humoured and round; but his nose, the rudder of the face, the index of the will, was small, feeble, nothing—like what he has done. It might seem that the genius of his face as from a height surveyed and projected him (with sufficient capacity and huge aspiration) into the world unknown of thought and imagination, with nothing to support or guide his veering purpose, as if Columbus had launched his adventurous course for the New World in a scallop, without oars or compass.

The contradiction that is overt in these accounts is implicit in a number of Coleridge's poems. In 1794, at a time when he was writing a great deal, we find him describing with a rhetorical flourish the gifts that Heaven has assigned him: "Energic Reason and a shaping mind,/ The daring ken of Truth, the Patriot's part," but all, he concluded, are "sloth-jaundic'd." And in a poetic address to his brother George he dwells with complacent melancholy on the prospect of himself, sad of soul, roaming, a stranger, through life. In the poem "To Two Sisters" there is a more sharply focused self-portrait:

Me disinherited in form and face
By nature, and mishap of outward grace;
Who, soul and body, through one guiltless fault
Waste daily with the poison of sad thought. . . .

The self-depreciation, a casual reader would assume, is fairly consistent. Yet there is an obvious contradiction between the character paralyzed by sloth, lost in painful reverie, and the poet who produces (in quite respectable quantity) this eloquent, often vigorous verse. Coleridge, I think, would have us aware of this opposition; as a writer he conceived on some level of consciousness the intention not to describe himself so much as to create a poetic character that embodies certain truths as to the way men act and respond. This exploitation of a more or less fictional self for dramatic purposes is one of the traits of Romantic poetry. The triumphant example of Coleridge's practice is the great ode, "Dejection," in which the "I" of the poem suffers and expresses the contraries of joy and despair, feeling and freezing thought, love and emotional emptiness. An equally clear, and simpler, example is "A Tombless Epitaph" in which the character who suffers a kind of death in life bears one of Coleridge's pen names, Idoloclastes Satyrane. "Mingling blame with praise," the poet explicitly balances the oppositions that are merely suggested in the first-person poems, and here we are firmly led to a judgment that we are, perhaps, meant to arrive at independently in other contexts:

Sickness, 'tis true,
Whole years of weary days, besieged him close,
Even to the gates and inlets of his life!
But it is true, no less, that strenuous, firm,
And with a natural gladness, he maintained

> The citadel unconquered, and in joy
> Was strong to follow the delightful Muse.
> For not a hidden path, that to the shades
> Of the beloved Parnassian forest leads,
> Lurked undiscovered by him; not a rill
> There issues from the fount of Hippocrene,
> But he had traced it upward to its source. . . .

The construction of such character images, or masks, though it is essential to all reflective poetry, has often been misinterpreted by readers. Lyrical poetry (other than pure song) must issue from a speaking voice, and the interest and richness of the poetry is usually enhanced when this voice has a certain dramatic complexity. But perhaps because the Romantic writers put such stress on the virtue of "sincerity," or it may be because of the general admiration for "realistic" literature, there has been a tendency in the last century or so to confuse the "I" in a poem with the poet himself. In the case of such a writer as Byron it is not difficult to discern the error of such confusion: the Byronic protagonist is painted in with such bold strokes that we can see what is going on. We now know that the identification of Lord Byron with Childe Harold, or speculations as to the degree to which the poetic character is the poet himself are, in a way, irrelevant. With a less flamboyant character, such as the poet who speaks in Coleridge's verse, the desire to read the poems as straight autobiography dies harder. The image of Coleridge wasting daily "with the poison of sad thought," still looms in many readers' and (more unfortunately) many writers' minds.

Yet this carefully constructed character of the poet dissipating his talents in reverie or escaping from sadness into abstruse research is pathetic in an artistic sense, and consequently vigorous and fertile. This *persona* is central to a body of reflective poems which may be said to deal with the activities of the mind in its relations to the external universe. The speaker, effective perhaps simply because he suffers dully so many of the normal human inadequacies, is the actor in an unerringly directed exploration into the process of thinking-perceiving. If we are to do justice to the poetry we must regard this "Coleridge" not as material for patronizing biographical insights, but as a lyrical protagonist whose power arises from his universality, who is representative of the conflict within every man between clogging self-absorption and free thought, pure mind and the dross of body.

To assert that the image of the poet that arises from his poems should be appreciated as a literary construction and seen in a dramatic perspective is not to deny the validity of biographical study. The real life of Samuel Taylor Coleridge is a permanently rewarding subject of analysis. But I believe that the interest and, let us say, dignity of many of the poems will be increased if they are read in their own frame of reference rather than as documents of a grand and muddled life.

In trying to find a way into the work of a poet one of the first questions to ask is, what lines of development does it show? Coleridge's poetry appears erratic; it may be said to display a number of leaps into excellence rather than a steady advance in poetic methods. In the earliest verse there is not much to arrest even the most favorably disposed reader. He followed the approved course for young poets of the late eighteenth century: there is imitation of Ossian, a good deal of melancholy posturing, some amorous poetry (that Coleridge himself later described as "of the namby-pamby genus"), and a number of diffuse lines concerned with various aspects of external nature. The poetry is uninteresting, not because it is in the eighteenth-century manner, but because its language, made up of the second-hand formulas of that manner, is lacking in concentration. The versifier who writes of "Noontide's sultry beam," and of the "skiey deluge" is not experiencing nature, but trying, rather, to describe experiences which he thinks he ought to have had.

The change, with a notable access of poetic vigor, comes when Coleridge is seized by an idea. In 1794 he and his friend Robert Southey projected a Utopian scheme, Pantisocracy, which, though superficially like many projects of undergraduate idealism, became something rich in Coleridge's mind. The plan was for twelve gentlemen "of good education and liberal principles" to embark with twelve ladies for the Susquehanna valley, there to establish a communistic settlement. It was assumed that with a good government and in a noble environment, evil would wither away. As Coleridge said in his sonnet, "Pantisocracy":

> O'er the ocean swell
> Sublime of Hope, I see the cottag'd dell
> Where Virtue calm with careless step may stray,
> And dancing to the moonlight roundelay,
> The wizard Passions weave an holy spell.

This dream of an ideal life has its ridiculous aspects, but it was for Coleridge (as Stephen Potter has acutely observed) something other than a mere *notion*. "It was what [he] was later to call a Principle. The first Idea in his life." His reaction to this unworkable and philosophically feeble plan shows Coleridge's faculty of being possessed by an intellectual passion. Naïve as it was, the plan became an organizing center of his sensibility. His own description of how one should respond to an idea is illuminating: "It is not enough that we have once swallowed it. The heart should have fed upon the truth, as insects on a leaf, till it be tinged with the color, and show its food in every [*sic*] the minutest fibre." This appetency is the very quality of his spirit and one of the sources of his poetic virtue.

The achievement of genuine poetry coincided in Coleridge's career with his abandonment of mechanistic systems of philosophy. In his younger days he had proudly described himself as a "complete necessitarean [*sic*]," and adhered to the associationist psychology of David Hartley. His attempts in prose and poetry to analyze his own experience seem to have led him away from eighteenth-century systems. In the most ambitious of his youthful philosophical poems, "The Destiny of Nations" (1796), we find him objecting to those who "chain down the wingèd thought, scoffing ascent," and those who cheat themselves

> With noisy emptiness of learned phrase,
> Their subtle fluids, impacts, essences,
> Self-working tools, uncaused effects, and all
> Those blind Omniscients, those Almighty Slaves,
> Untenanting creation of its God.

He admires those bold enough to think,

> That as one body seems the aggregate
> Of atoms numberless, each organized;
> So by a strange and dim similitude
> Infinite myriads of self-conscious minds
> Are one all-conscious Spirit, which informs
> With absolute ubiquity of thought
> (His one eternal self-affirming act!)
> All his involvèd Monads. . . .

The verse is muddy, but the speculations it expresses lead directly to the great poems. By 1801 Coleridge had given up the sect of Locke, "a perfect Little-ist," for a transcendental philosophy:

> My opinion is thus: that deep thinking is attainable only by a man of deep feeling, and that all truth is a species of revelation. The more I understand of Sir Isaac Newton's works, the more boldly I dare to utter my own mind, . . . that I believe the souls of five hundred Sir Isaac Newtons would go to the making up of a Shakespeare or a Milton.

Though Coleridge—almost an archetype of the inquiring spirit—never ceased to develop philosophically, one has the feeling in regard to his poetry that once the leap from mechanistic notions to intuitionism has been made his poetic development is accomplished. There is, after this change, diversity of interest and accomplishment; his poetic powers are in some respects deepened, in others dissipated, but there is no development along definable lines. In attempting, then, to draw out the salient features of

Coleridge's poetry it is better to consider, not development, but recurrent themes that link diverse poems to a common center, and then go on to distinguish the kinds of poetry he achieved.

"The Eolian Harp," chronologically the first really good poem, introduces the most important of the reiterated themes. The wind harp, the breeze that blows through it and the irregular music that rises from it furnish the three elements of Coleridge's first adequate symbol of the imaginative process, of the harmonies of thought and feeling that create ideas. The conceptual foundation of "The Eolian Harp" is suggested in a letter to Southey:

> I almost think that ideas *never* recall ideas, as far as they are ideas, any more than leaves in a forest create each other's motion. The breeze it is that runs through them—it is the soul, the state of feeling.

In "The Eolian Harp" the realization of this idea takes place dramatically. The music first leads the tranquil poet-speaker to reflect on the interfusion of natural forms:

> O! the one Life within us and abroad,
> Which meets all motion and becomes its soul,
> A light in sound, a sound-like power in light,
> Rhythm in all thought, and joyance every where—
> Methinks it should have been impossible
> Not to love all things in a world so fill'd;
> Where the breeze warbles, and the mute still air
> Is Music slumbering on her instrument.*

The harp may symbolize the living mind played upon by soul, but such a conception does not go far enough in realizing the reciprocities of nature. In his attempt to express in the language of symbol the power of the mind both to create and to be created by outward nature, the poet's speculations became bolder. "What if," he asks,

* This passage was not in the original version of the poem.

> all of animated nature
> Be but organic Harps diversely fram'd,
> That tremble into thought, as o'er them sweeps
> Plastic and vast, one intellectual breeze,
> At once the Soul of each, and God of all?

But this is to go too far. He accepts the reproof of his beloved companion's "more serious eye" and, chastened, describes his speculation as one of the bubbles that "rise and break/ On vain Philosophy's aye-babbling spring." The poem ends with a diminuendo that returns us to everyday reality.

There has been much confusion as to the meaning of Coleridge's conclusion. Readers have not always seen why the "shapings of the unregenerate mind" from which the poet so promptly withdraws are inconsistent with Christian humility and a "Faith that inly *feels*" (as the concluding lines of the poem suggest). May it not be, however, that in this poem about the expressive powers of the imagination the poet is suggesting the inadequacy of an elevated speculation which is not in harmony with the situation into which it is introduced? If it were a genuine, whole perception it would rise out of and be interfused with the religious feeling of his beloved, their cottage, and the things around them.

In "The Nightingale" the breeze is again a dominant motif. In this poem the bird, traditionally the symbol of the poet, is—what the harp has been in other poems—the harmonious voice of vital nature. The Lady, "vowed and dedicate/ To something more than Nature," has been privileged to see the flock of nightingales wakened by the moon,

> and those wakeful birds
> Have all burst forth in choral minstrelsy,
> As if some sudden gale had swept at once
> A hundred airy harps!

The same theme is important in "Fears in Solitude," in which the young man who has allowed the sweet influences "from the sun, and from the breezy air" to tremble "o'er his frame" is a kind of Aeolian harp whose music is a dream. In Coleridge's finest political poem, "France: An Ode," the breeze image is transformed and extended without losing its essential connotations. The Revolution is conceived of as a storm. In the conclusion of the ode the poet evokes a spirit of Liberty whose manifestations are above and apart from the actions of perturbed and rebellious men. This preternatural influence is the guide of winds, felt by the tranquil man as the breeze that informs the solitudes of nature.

The latest and most complex use of the wind-harp image is in "Dejection." At the beginning of the poem the atmospheric depression preceding a storm symbolizes (or *is*) the spiritual state of the poet; the intellectual breeze has become a "dull sobbing draft." To the soul that is dead to joy harmonious nature is inanimate and cold. The poet whose shaping spirit of imagination is suspended, is heedless of the freshening wind, but it is that variable storm-wind of the last two sections of the poem that offers the fullest embodiment of Coleridge's conception of the reconciliation of suffering and joy, destruction and creation, of his sense of the interpenetration of man's inner life with the life of nature—insights which he achieved only partially in earlier poems.

The kinds of realization that Coleridge's recurrent wind images are designed to effect suggest that he was writing poetry that did not fit into the current and approved categories of the late eighteenth century. The odes, perhaps, are not novel in form, though they are in subject matter; but such poems as "The Eolian Harp," "Fears in Solitude," "The Nightingale," to cite only a few examples, are decidedly not descriptive or reflective poems in any traditional sense. They treat of the imagination, not in the manner of self-involved introspection that was to become characteristic of later Romantic poetry, but in a way that achieves a philosophical assertion by means of poetic vision. They may be said to deal with the problem of knowledge. In probing the relations between mind and experience Coleridge developed an appropriate poetic form, one that had been anticipated in earlier poetry (Cowper's "Task" comes closest to it) but of which he is the true originator. The term which he used to describe "The Nightingale," a "conversation poem," is the best label for the group which includes, among others, "This Lime-Tree Bower My Prison," "Frost at Midnight," "Fears in Solitude," and "To William Wordsworth." In all these poems the poet, placed in a humble, everyday situation, is imagined to be the speaker. The simple diction evokes the rhythms of ordinary speech; and much of the beauty of the conversation poems is in their tone of natural feeling which rises only to a muted eloquence. It is not the least of Coleridge's achievements that in this admirable group of poems he captures more successfully than Wordsworth (who issued manifestoes on the subject) a sense of "the real language of men."

More is seminal in these poems, however, than the exploitation of natural diction. Their pattern is both original and significant to poetry that was to follow. In commenting on his deletion of the original six-line conclusion to "Frost at Midnight," Coleridge said that he had decided to omit the lines because "they destroy the rondo, and return upon itself of the Poem. A Poem of this kind of length ought to be coiled with its tail round its head." He was no doubt thinking primarily of the desirability of concluding his poem with an echo of its magnificent first line, "The Frost performs its secret ministry," but this return of the poem upon itself occurs also on the level of the metaphorical action of "Frost at Midnight," and of several other poems.

The typical procedure is for the poet-speaker to be presented in a situation of ordinary life which contains and directs his reflections and memories. "Frost at Midnight" is the paradigm: the poem opens with the poet sitting in front of the fire in his cottage late on a cold night, with his infant child sleeping in a cradle beside him. He contemplates the fire, then moving out from his own hearth, considers the village around him and the great world beyond that. His mind returns to the fire; he regards the thin film of flame on the grate, and imagines that it may be a "companionable form" infused by the Spirit which seeks everywhere an "Echo or mirror" of itself. The peculiar flame on the grate leads him, with a rush of recollection, to memories of his schooldays and of the superstition connected with such films of flame. Then, breaking off this reverie, he turns to the sleeping infant and, with mounting eloquence, prays that his child shall hear:

> that eternal language, which thy God
> Utters, who from eternity doth teach
> Himself in all, and all things in himself.
> Great universal Teacher! he shall mould
> Thy spirit, and by giving make it ask.

But the poem has its tail round its head; in the concluding lines it drops back to the cottage kitchen and the frost at midnight, to that quiet center which is the source of visionary joy.

The design of such a poem follows and stylizes the dilatory movements of the poet's mind. The reader moves with the poetic speaker to heightened awareness and, with him, sinks back into quietude. The form is also a three-fold one which reflects in an unobtrusive way the dialectical pattern of organic growth. The rondo form may be described as A B A; but the A to which we return after the experience of B is permanently modified: the relation between the two A's of a Coleridge poem resembles that between the thesis and synthesis of the dialectical progression. Though there is nothing intrinsically more *natural* in this structure than in, say, the apostrophes to nature in descriptive poems of the earlier eighteenth century, the reader feels more directly involved in the activity of the poem. The form gives a sense of dramatic reality and persuades us that we have been, not presented with the polished product of the poet's cogitation, but rather asked to follow him in his explorations of consciousness. It is a further virtue of the form that its effect of immediacy, its presentation of a character in a realized setting, enable the poet to attach what might in other circumstances be too abstract speculation to a concrete matrix. We can more easily apprehend the prospect of a man thinking than we can take in a naked idea.

In the conversation or "rondo" poems Coleridge arrived at a form essentially dramatic in its effect. However, the odes, "Dejection" and "France," though they belong to a more formal genre, exploit the same dramatic pattern. In both odes there is a defined center from which the poetic reflection moves out, and in both a return of the poet's mind upon itself. The general qualities of this design—which Coleridge was the first to employ effectively—have strongly influenced the practice of several distinguished poets who followed him. Matthew Arnold, for example, made continued use of a structure in which the poet finds himself in a situation, not remarkable, but presenting features that provoke lyric reflection. In his poems the thought moves out from the concrete, back and forth in time, and returns to its starting point. Later W. B. Yeats made striking use of the device: in such a poem as "Among School Children" we seem to follow the random movements of the poet's mind as an everyday experience leads him to recollection and impassioned meditation. An important feature of this pattern, and one that is apparent in Coleridge's use of it, is that it makes the whole poem a metaphor of the activity of the poetic sensibility—a process which is peculiarly appropriate to Coleridge's intense psychological interest and, more widely, to the Romantic aesthetic with its concentration on individual experience and on the details of ordinary life.

Perhaps the most celebrated genre of Romantic literature is what is loosely called nature poetry. Though it may be wise to consider his treatment of nature more a poetic faculty manifesting itself in all his verse than a special category, Coleridge is undoubtedly in the first rank of "nature poets." There is some confusion as to what that term finally means, but on the simplest level most of the Romantic poets, Coleridge included, were in some sense "nature lovers." They liked the outdoors, took long walks and appreciated views. Not the least significant of Coleridge's contributions to intellectual history is his quite novel love of mountain and rock climbing. Mount Scafell, the scene of his first exploits, was no Matterhorn, but his description of the techniques and gratifications of climbing is half a century ahead of the Victorian outburst of mountaineering enthusiasm. Coleridge began with simple enjoyment of the natural world. He wrote to his brother:

> I love fields and woods and mountains with an almost visionary fondness. And because I have found benevolence and quietness growing within me as that fondness has increased, therefore I should wish to be the means of implanting it in others.

This is a clear statement of the elementary Romantic notion of nature as a source of value and of healing power. But such uncomplicated convictions make naturalists, not poets; for Coleridge the task was to move, step by step, up the scale of perception. He first translated his enthusiasm into attempts at precise expression. The "verdant hills" and stars with "chaste effulgent glow" of the earliest poems give way to painstaking description. Coleridge spoke delightedly of Dorothy Wordsworth having an eye, "watchful in minutest observation of nature." The phrase characterizes his own powers. He was wont to remind friends who considered him a metaphysician that he took "delight in little things." He speaks of himself as "making studies" as a painter might, and the notebooks are full of verbal transcriptions:

> Black round Ink-spots from 5 to 18 in the decaying leaf of the Sycamore.
> A circular glade in a forest of Birch Trees, and in the center of the circle, a stone standing upright, twice a tall man's Height—and by its side a stately Ash Tree umbrellaing it.—

The notes to the poems frequently indicate the pains he took to get natural details just right. When, for example, he uses as a simile the flashing effect of marigolds at dusk:

'Tis said, in Summer's evening hour
Flashes the golden-colour'd flower
    A fair electric flame,

he speculated at length in a footnote on the incidences and cause of the phenomenon. In "Inscription for a Fountain on a Heath" a vivid passage,

                    Nor ever cease
Yon tiny cone of sand its soundless dance,
Which at the bottom, like a Fairy's Page,
As merry and no taller, dances still,
Nor wrinkles the smooth surface of the Fount.

is transposed from a notebook entry:

The spring with the little tiny cone of loose sand ever rising and sinking at the bottom, but it's [sic] surface without a wrinkle.

In "This Lime-Tree Bower My Prison" Coleridge finds the exact and unforgettable word to express the sound made by the rook's wings in flight. A delight in descriptive exactness informs the visionary poems as well as the poems of nature. In a lengthy note to line 104 of "The Ancient Mariner" the poet describes his effort to arrive at the verb that would accurately convey the appearance of the furrowed wake streaming off behind a ship. Indeed, an important element of the reader's responses to that poem, and to "Christabel" and to "Kubla Khan" as well, rises from the conjunction of a supernatural narrative and a magical world with the utmost exactness of physical detail.

Coleridge's significance as the initial practitioner in poetry of a disciplined, minute observation has never been properly assessed. For reasons that have not been explained, an interest in the precise rendering of external nature came to dominate English poetry and painting in the nineteenth century. Tennyson, the Pre-Raphaelites,

Gerard Manley Hopkins trained their vision to catch the subtlest distinctions of color and form, and worked to convey in words or in paint the exact equivalent of a visual and tactile impression. This artistic concern is clearly related to the tendencies in literature and painting that are called "realism," and, less directly, to the social interests of a democratic age. Essentially, however, it represents a fertilization of the arts by technology and by what is most vital in the procedures of the natural sciences. Both in England and in France there was a conscious attempt on the part of literary and visual artists to make some bridge between their realms of discourse and the increasingly imposing areas of scientific investigation. Coleridge, with his usual prescience, made this connection quite early; in describing the activity of his friend, the chemist Sir Humphry Davy, and of two other English scientists, he was impelled to compare their work with that of the greatest of literary artists:

> If in Shakespeare we find nature idealized into poetry through the creative power of a profound yet observant meditation, so through the meditative observation of a Davy, a Wollaston, or a Hatchett . . . we find poetry, as it were, substantiated and realized in nature. . . .

For the poet accuracy of vision is not enough, the perception of natural forms not an end in itself. For Coleridge, to look is to speculate:

> —Hung over the Bridge, & musing considering how much of this Scene of endless variety in Identity was Nature's—how much the living organ's!—What would it be if I had the eyes of a fly!—what if the blunt eye of a Brobdignag!—

His best nature poems pose these questions in many subtle ways. He essays to make the external internal:

> In looking at objects of Nature while I am thinking, as at yonder moon dim-glimmering through the dewy

window-pane, I seem rather to be seeking, as it were *asking* for, a symbolical language for something within me that already and for ever exists.

And yet (Coleridge forces us to ever finer distinctions) the symbolic aspect is not adumbrated by simile or moralization. In the rare moments when the Romantic poet transcends—or goes deeper than—the poetic operations of the Metaphysicals' analogies or the moral parallelisms of eighteenth-century nature poetry, we see that his vision is capable of providing an insight of unprecedented acuity and wholeness. In the nature poetry of his immediate predecessors—particularly Cowper and Bowles— Coleridge found much to admire; but he saw also what was defective in their practice. In a brilliant letter of 1802 he objected to Bowles' habit of "moralizing everything,"

> never to see or describe any interesting appearance in nature without connecting it, by dim analogies, with the moral world proves faintness of impression. Nature has her proper interest, and he will know what it is who believes and feels that everything has a life of its own, and that we are all *One Life*. A poet's heart and intellect should be *combined*, intimately combined and unified with the great appearances of nature, and not merely held in solution and loose mixture with them, in the shape of formal similes.

The passage might stand as an epigraph to all of Coleridge's poetry. Implied in it is the aesthetic philosophy which Ruskin was to make current later in the century: for Ruskin the highest form of perception resulted from an intuitive leap which could occur when the perceiver submitted himself to the clearest and most loving observation of natural detail. Well into the twentieth century an elaborate set of theories on the nature of art and poetry derived from this principle which Coleridge so fully expressed.

Seen in detachment, another class of Coleridge's poetry may help us to recognize his achievement. The psychological poems rise from personal experience and treat the subjects of melancholy and unrequited love. Many poets —particularly since the time of Rousseau—have found their material in their internal suffering. Moods of dejection do, in fact, provide so many opportunities for easy poetizing that they become the stock-in-trade of petty versifiers. But if we compare the appropriate poems of Coleridge with even the finest examples of Romantic Melancholy we see that he is doing something quite different: he is not just posturing, but really saying something about human suffering. A terrible passage from the *Notebooks* is relevant here:

> I write melancholy, always melancholy: you will suspect that it is the fault of my natural Temper. Alas! no.—This is the great Cross in that my Nature is made for Joy—impelling me to Joyance—& I never —never can yield to it.—I am a genuine *Tantalus*—

Perhaps because he loved the power of joy he was able to consider melancholy in a fresh way. The poetic language in which he records depressed states of mind has a concentration, an intensity, that is rarely to be found in the work of his contemporaries. The theme is so persistent as to be almost at the heart of his work. "Dejection" is the representative poem, but others have their special interest: "The Pains of Sleep" and the fragment, "The Night-Mare Death in Life," foreshadow the account of spiritual agony in Hopkins' "terrible" sonnets. Of another group of poems that describe with eloquence and candor the loss of creative power, "Work without Hope" and "To William Wordsworth" are perhaps the most interesting.

Also in the category of psychological poetry and closely related in feeling to the poems of melancholy is the important group of love poems from Coleridge's middle and later career. Most of this poetry centers on his deep but hopeless love for Sara Hutchinson, Wordsworth's sister-in-law and the "Asra" of the poems, whom he met in 1799. The poem "Love," the first record of this meeting, portrays the situation by means of a symbolic narrative. In many other verses, some of them fragmentary, the poet went on to define explicitly his emotional state; the sonnet "To Asra" is notable: addressing the woman "beyond utterance dear," he describes a love which,

> ever welling at my heart,
> Now in its living fount doth heave and fall,
> Now overflowing pours thro' every part
> Of all my frame, and fills and changes all. . . .

The original version of "Dejection" was sent in a letter to Sara Hutchinson, and it was she who was addressed in the poem. The grief the poet describes, it must be emphasized, is not merely for the loss of his "shaping spirit of Imagination," but for the impossibility of joining his beloved. In succeeding years such poems as "The Picture," "Phantom," "Recollections of Love," and such fragments as "I have experienced the worst the world can wreak on me," touch in many different ways on the deprivation of love. A recurrent note is struck in the line, "Why was I made for Love and Love denied to me?"

As even casual quotation suggests, there is a strong flavor of self-pity in these poems, but they are redeemed by Coleridge's permanent toughness of intellect. As time went on, he seems to have become less concerned with his frustration than with the nature of love itself. In a fascinating letter of 1811 he reflects on the impossibility of one who has not been in love understanding what love is, and suggests that the body "in her homely way . . . tries to interpret all the movements of the Soul." Several of the later poems are subtle analyses of the workings of passion as well as despairing laments at love's loss:

> In many ways does the full heart reveal
> The presence of the love it would conceal;

But in far more the estrangéd heart lets know
The absence of the love, which yet it fain would
shew.

It would be easy to over-estimate Coleridge's love
poems, but since his accomplishment in this genre has
been almost completely ignored, it is worth pointing out
that at times he achieves that rare thing, lyric love poetry
that is touched with the tragic spirit. Some of his work
is worthy of comparison with Hardy's poems on the death
of his wife or the Maud Gonne poems of Yeats. "Love's
Apparition and Evanishment," with its wry reflection on
the inevitable accession of the conquering cold, is representative of the whole group of late love poems:

> In vain we supplicate the Powers above;
> There is no resurrection for the Love
> That, nursed in tenderest care, yet fades away
> In the chill'd heart by gradual self-decay.

That there is yet another, and conspicuously non-lyrical,
category of Coleridge's poetry is further evidence of his
versatility. In the same year in which he completed "The
Ancient Mariner" and "Frost at Midnight," he wrote the
political poem "France." There are no other verses on pol-
itics that can be compared with this ode, but there is a
respectable number of vigorous historical poems and epigrams on various subjects which, along with "France,"
make up a definable group. The reader who knows only
the "magic" Coleridge will be surprised by "Lines Suggested by the Last Words of Berengarius," a poem which
displays an interesting combination of the informal diction perfected in the conversation poems with rhymed
couplets of an almost Augustan regularity. It is a poem
of statement, in the plain style, treating the subject of
individual conscience and historical change. Coleridge's
epigrams—"On Donne's Poetry," "Truth I Pursued," "Cologne"—are not major works; but it is no exaggeration
to say that he is the best English epigrammatist after

Jonson and Sir John Harington. His experiments in a form that requires such wit and rhetorical resource are impressive examples of the perpetual coruscation of his spirit.

The reader who has agreed to follow this division of Coleridge's poetry into several overlapping but distinguishable groups will by now have observed that the three most important poems have barely been mentioned. In fact "The Ancient Mariner," "Christabel," and "Kubla Khan" do not fit under any heading so far defined, and would have to be grouped in a special category of "visionary" poems. It is generally conceded that, with the exception of some poems of Blake, they are the finest examples in our language of their class of poetry. Nevertheless, they have been intentionally omitted from this brief discussion simply because I think they have already received an adequate amount of attention and analysis. Indeed, it is hard to think of any poems in English literature that have been so promptly, so widely, and so consistently appreciated. Their celebrity has tended to overshadow—at times completely—Coleridge's other poetry. My purpose is not so much to de-emphasize the three great poems as to suggest, by directing attention to the other poetry, that they are not mutants, separable from the staple of the poet's work. Actually, our admiration of the visionary poems is likely to be increased if we see them rising out of a body of sustained creative effort. Of "The Ancient Mariner" and "Christabel" particularly, it can be said that they are great because they contain and extend the diverse interests of many lesser poems, because they realize the insights hinted at in other works.

If there is any general quality which characterizes all of Coleridge's work, it is the sense of a continual extension of thought and perception. The Romantic movement can almost (perhaps, can only) be defined as the exploration and occasional conquest of new territories of experience. Coleridge pushes these conquests farther than the other Romantics had done. There are, for example, many nineteenth-century ballads concerning the visitation of demon ladies, but "Christabel" is so many things in addition that its meanings can never be specified. "The Ancient Mariner" is not original in form, but its descriptive precision, its exploitation of archetypal motifs, its symbolic complexity make it the apotheosis of its form.

Coleridge was not, like Milton, or Pope, or even Tennyson, a lord of language. He lacked their ability to create lines with a cadence or turn that give them an unmistakable stamp. Because he did not often enough fuse the various elements of his inspiration into a coherent structure he was not a great poet. But he was never a *minor* poet: in everything he wrote in his maturity there is richness and excitement. With the alteration of only one word it is entirely just to say of him what he so finely said of Milton: that he "wrote nothing without an interior meaning. 'Where more is meant than meets the ear,' is true of him beyond [most] other writers."

G. ROBERT STANGE
March 1959

BIBLIOGRAPHY

The standard edition is *The Poems of Samuel Taylor Coleridge*, edited by E. H. Coleridge, 2 vols., 1912. The best edition of *Biographia Literaria* is that edited by J. Shawcross, 2 vols., 1907. The sumptuous edition of the *Notebooks* by Kathleen Coburn, 1956- is still appearing, as are the *Collected Letters*, edited by E. L. Griggs, 1956-.

James Dykes Campbell's *Coleridge: A Narrative of the Events of His Life*, 1894, is a straightforward biography. An interesting biographical essay is Stephen Potter, *Coleridge and S.T.C.*, 1935. Some of the more influential critical works are, J. L. Lowes, *The Road to Xanadu*, revised edition, 1930; I. A. Richards, *Coleridge on Imagination*, revised edition, 1950; and Humphry House, *Coleridge*, 1953.

Chronology

1772 Samuel Taylor Coleridge born October 21, at Ottery St. Mary, Devonshire.

1782 Coleridge entered Christ's Hospital school at London.

1791 He matriculated at Jesus College, Cambridge.

1793 He enlisted in the Light Dragoons in December.

1794 Discharged from Dragoons by intervention of friends, returned to Cambridge in April.
In June he met Southey at Oxford, formed the scheme of Pantisocracy.
In December he left Cambridge for good.

1795 In January delivered political lectures at Bristol (published as *Conciones ad Populum, Or Addresses to the People*). Met Wordsworth. On October 4, married to Sarah Fricker.

1796 Published periodical, *The Watchman*, and *Poems on Various Subjects*.
Hartley Coleridge born on September 19.
In December the family settled at Nether Stowey.

1797 The Wordsworths moved to Alfoxden in order to be near Coleridge.
Poems, by S. T. Coleridge, Second Edition published in June.
November 13, "Ancient Mariner" begun.

1798 Received from the Wedgwood brothers an annuity of 150 pounds.

Lyrical Ballads published in September.
In September Coleridge and the Wordsworths sailed for Germany.

1799 He spent the autumn in the Lake District, and there met Sara Hutchinson.

1800 In July the family settled at Greta Hall, Keswick. Derwent Coleridge born September 14.

1802 Sara Coleridge born December 23.

1804 In April Coleridge went to Malta for his health.

1806 In August he returned to England, but from this time on was permanently, though not formally, separated from his wife.

1808 He delivered his first lectures at the Royal Institution.

1809 From June to March, 1810, he published *The Friend*.

1810 He broke with Wordsworth.
In the years between 1810 and 1816 he lectured at London and at Bristol, revised his play, *Osorio*, which was produced in 1813 as *Remorse*, and was partially reconciled with Wordsworth.

1816 In April went to live with James Gillman and his wife at Highgate, where he stayed for the rest of his life.
In June published "Christabel" and "Kubla Khan."

1817 Published the second *Lay Sermon*, *Biographia Literaria*, *Sibylline Leaves*, and *Zapolya*.

1818 From December to March, 1819, lectured on the history of philosophy.

1825 *Aids to Reflection* published.

1828 *Poetical Works* (three volumes) published.

1830 Published the *Constitution of Church and State*.

1834 Coleridge died on July 25.

To the Rev. W. L. Bowles

[SECOND VERSION]

My heart has thank'd thee, BOWLES! for those soft
   strains *
  Whose sadness soothes me, like the murmuring
  Of wild-bees in the sunny showers of spring!
For hence not callous to the mourner's pains

Through Youth's gay prime and thornless paths I went:
  And when the mightier Throes of mind began,
  And drove me forth, a thought-bewilder'd man,
Their mild and manliest melancholy lent

A mingled charm, such as the pang consign'd
  To slumber, though the big tear it renew'd;   10
  Bidding a strange mysterious PLEASURE brood
Over the wavy and tumultuous mind,

As the great SPIRIT erst with plastic sweep
Mov'd on the darkness of the unform'd deep.

The Eolian Harp

COMPOSED AT CLEVEDON, SOMERSETSHIRE

My pensive Sara! thy soft cheek reclined *
Thus on mine arm, most soothing sweet it is
To sit beside our Cot, our Cot o'ergrown
With white-flower'd Jasmin, and the broad-leav'd Myrtle,
(Meet emblems they of Innocence and Love!)
And watch the clouds, that late were rich with light,
Slow saddening round, and mark the star of eve
Serenely brilliant (such should Wisdom be)
Shine opposite! How exquisite the scents

* An asterisk refers to the notes which begin on p. 153.

Snatch'd from yon bean-field! and the world *so* hush'd!
The stilly murmur of the distant Sea   11
Tells us of silence.
                    And that simplest Lute,
Placed length-ways in the clasping casement, hark!
How by the desultory breeze caress'd,
Like some coy maid half yielding to her lover,
It pours such sweet upbraiding, as must needs
Tempt to repeat the wrong! And now, its strings
Boldlier swept, the long sequacious notes
Over delicious surges sink and rise,
Such a soft floating witchery of sound   20
As twilight Elfins make, when they at eve
Voyage on gentle gales from Fairy-Land,
Where Melodies round honey-dropping flowers,
Footless and wild, like birds of Paradise,
Nor pause, nor perch, hovering on untam'd wing!
O! the one Life within us and abroad,
Which meets all motion and becomes its soul,
A light in sound, a sound-like power in light,
Rhythm in all thought, and joyance every where—
Methinks, it should have been impossible   30
Not to love all things in a world so fill'd;
Where the breeze warbles, and the mute still air
Is Music slumbering on her instrument.

    And thus, my Love! as on the midway slope
Of yonder hill I stretch my limbs at noon,
Whilst through my half-clos'd eye-lids I behold
The sunbeams dance, like diamonds, on the main,
And tranquil muse upon tranquillity;
Full many a thought uncall'd and undetain'd,
And many idle flitting phantasies,   40
Traverse my indolent and passive brain,
As wild and various as the random gales
That swell and flutter on this subject Lute!
    And what if all of animated nature
Be but organic Harps diversely fram'd,
That tremble into thought, as o'er them sweeps

                            [*The Eolian Harp*] 36

Plastic and vast, one intellectual breeze,
At once the Soul of each, and God of all?
　But thy more serious eye a mild reproof
Darts, O belovéd Woman! nor such thoughts　　　　50
Dim and unhallow'd dost thou not reject,
And biddest me walk humbly with my God.
Meek Daughter in the family of Christ!
Well hast thou said and holily disprais'd
These shapings of the unregenerate mind;
Bubbles that glitter as they rise and break
On vain Philosophy's aye-babbling spring.
For never guiltless may I speak of him,
The Incomprehensible! save when with awe
I praise him, and with Faith that inly *feels;*　　　60
Who with his saving mercies healéd me,
A sinful and most miserable man,
Wilder'd and dark, and gave me to possess
Peace, and this Cot, and thee, heart-honour'd Maid!

The Raven

A CHRISTMAS TALE, T LD BY A SCHOOL-BOY
TO HIS LITTLE BROTH RS AND SISTERS

Underneath an old oak tree *
There was of swine a huge company,
That grunted as they crunched the mast:
For that was ripe, and fell full fast.
Then they trotted away, for the wind grew high:
One acorn they left, and no more might you spy.
Next came a Raven, that liked not such folly:
He belonged, they did say, to the witch Melancholy!
Blacker was he than blackest jet,
Flew low in the rain, and his feathers not wet.　　　10
He picked up the acorn and buried it straight
By the side of a river both deep and great.
　　　Where then did the Raven go?
　　　He went high and low,

Over hill, over dale, did the black Raven go.
    Many Autumns, many Springs
    Travelled he with wandering wings:
    Many Summers, many Winters—
    I can't tell half his adventures.

At length he came back, and with him a She,   20
And the acorn was grown to a tall oak tree.
They built them a nest in the topmost bough,
And young ones they had, and were happy enow.
But soon came a Woodman in leathern guise,
His brow, like a pent-house, hung over his eyes.
He'd an axe in his hand, not a word he spoke,
But with many a hem! and a sturdy stroke,
At length he brought down the poor Raven's own oak.
His young ones were killed; for they could not depart,
And their mother did die of a broken heart.   30

The boughs from the trunk the Woodman did sever;
And they floated it down on the course of the river.
They sawed it in planks, and its bark they did strip,
And with this tree and others they made a good ship.
The ship, it was launched; but in sight of the land
Such a storm there did rise as no ship could withstand.
It bulged on a rock, and the waves rush'd in fast:
Round and round flew the raven, and cawed to the blast.
He heard the last shriek of the perishing souls—
See! see! o'er the topmast the mad water rolls!   40
    Right glad was the Raven, and off he went fleet,
And Death riding home on a cloud he did meet,
And he thank'd him again and again for this treat:
    They had taken his all, and REVENGE IT WAS SWEET!

This Lime-Tree Bower My Prison

[ADDRESSED TO CHARLES LAMB,
OF THE INDIA HOUSE, LONDON]

*In the June of 1797 some long-expected friends paid a
visit to the author's cottage; and on the morning of their
arrival, he met with an accident, which disabled him from
walking during the whole time of their stay. One evening,
when they had left him for a few hours, he composed the
following lines in the garden-bower.**

Well, they are gone, and here must I remain,
This lime-tree bower my prison! I have lost
Beauties and feelings, such as would have been
Most sweet to my remembrance even when age
Had dimm'd mine eyes to blindness! They, meanwhile,
Friends, whom I never more may meet again,
On springy heath, along the hill-top edge,
Wander in gladness, and wind down, perchance,
To that still roaring dell, of which I told;
The roaring dell, o'erwooded, narrow, deep,   10
And only speckled by the mid-day sun;
Where its slim trunk the ash from rock to rock
Flings arching like a bridge;—that branchless ash,
Unsunn'd and damp, whose few poor yellow leaves
Ne'er tremble in the gale, yet tremble still,
Fann'd by the water-fall! and there my friends
Behold the dark green file of long lank weeds,*
That all at once (a most fantastic sight!)
Still nod and drip beneath the dripping edge
Of the blue clay-stone.   20

                    Now, my friends emerge
Beneath the wide wide Heaven—and view again
The many-steepled tract magnificent
Of hilly fields and meadows, and the sea,
With some fair bark, perhaps, whose sails light up
The slip of smooth clear blue betwixt two Isles

Of purple shadow! Yes! they wander on
In gladness all; but thou, methinks, most glad,
My gentle-hearted Charles! for thou hast pined
And hunger'd after Nature, many a year,   30
In the great City pent, winning thy way
With sad yet patient soul, through evil and pain
And strange calamity! Ah! slowly sink
Behind the western ridge, thou glorious Sun!
Shine in the slant beams of the sinking orb,
Ye purple heath-flowers! richlier burn, ye clouds!
Live in the yellow light, ye distant groves!
And kindle, thou blue Ocean! So my friend
Struck with deep joy may stand, as I have stood,
Silent with swimming sense; yea, gazing round   40
On the wide landscape, gaze till all doth seem
Less gross than bodily; and of such hues
As veil the Almighty Spirit, when yet he makes
Spirits perceive his presence.

                    A delight
Comes sudden on my heart, and I am glad
As I myself were there! Nor in this bower,
This little lime-tree bower, have I not mark'd
Much that has sooth'd me. Pale beneath the blaze
Hung the transparent foliage; and I watch'd   50
Some broad and sunny leaf, and lov'd to see
The shadow of the leaf and stem above
Dappling its sunshine! And that walnut-tree
Was richly ting'd, and a deep radiance lay
Full on the ancient ivy, which usurps
Those fronting elms, and now, with blackest mass
Makes their dark branches gleam a lighter hue
Through the late twilight: and though now the bat
Wheels silent by, and not a swallow twitters,
Yet still the solitary humble-bee   60
Sings in the bean-flower! Henceforth I shall know
That Nature ne'er deserts the wise and pure;
No plot so narrow, be but Nature there,
No waste so vacant, but may well employ

                [*This Lime-Tree Bower My Prison*] 40

Each faculty of sense, and keep the heart
Awake to Love and Beauty! and sometimes
'Tis well to be bereft of promis'd good,
That we may lift the soul, and contemplate
With lively joy the joys we cannot share.
My gentle-hearted Charles! when the last rook   70
Beat its straight path along the dusky air
Homewards, I blest it! deeming its black wing
(Now a dim speck, now vanishing in light)
Had cross'd the mighty Orb's dilated glory,
While thou stood'st gazing; or, when all was still,
Flew creeking o'er thy head, and had a charm *
For thee, my gentle-hearted Charles, to whom
No sound is dissonant which tells of Life.

romantic

The Rime of the Ancient Mariner ✓

IN SEVEN PARTS

Facile credo, plures esse Naturas invisibiles quam visibiles in rerum universitate. Sed horum omnium familiam quis nobis enarrabit? et gradus et cognationes et discrimina et singulorum munera? Quid agunt? quae loca habitant? Harum rerum notitiam semper ambivit ingenium humanum, nunquam attigit. Juvat, interea, non diffiteor, quandoque in animo, tanquam in tabulà, majoris et melioris mundi imaginem contemplari: ne mens assuefacta hodiernae vitae minutiis se contrahat nimis, et tota subsidat in pusillas cogitationes. Sed veritati interea invigilandum est, modusque servandus, ut certa ab incertis, diem a nocte, distinguamus.

—T. BURNET, *Archaeol. Phil.* p. 68.*

ARGUMENT

How a Ship having passed the Line was driven by storms to the cold Country towards the South Pole; and how from thence she made her course to the tropical Latitude

of the Great Pacific Ocean; and of the strange things that
befell; and in what manner the Ancyent Marinere came
back to his own Country.

PART I

An ancient
Mariner meeteth
three Gallants
bidden to a
wedding-feast,
and detaineth
one.

It is an ancient Mariner,
And he stoppeth one of three.
"By thy long grey beard and glittering
  eye,
Now wherefore stopp'st thou me?

The Bridegroom's doors are opened wide,
And I am next of kin;
The guests are met, the feast is set:
May'st hear the merry din."

He holds him with his skinny hand,
"There was a ship," quoth he.   10
"Hold off! unhand me, grey-beard loon!"
Eftsoons his hand dropt he.

The Wedding-
Guest is
spellbound by
the eye of the old
seafaring man,
and constrained
to hear his tale.

He holds him with his glittering eye—
The Wedding-Guest stood still,
And listens like a three years' child:
The Mariner hath his will.

The Wedding-Guest sat on a stone:
He cannot choose but hear;
And thus spake on that ancient man,
The bright-eyed Mariner.   20

The ship was cheered, the harbour
  cleared,
The Mariner tells
how the ship
sailed southward
with a good
wind and fair
weather, till it
reached the line.
Merrily did we drop
Below the kirk, below the hill,
Below the lighthouse top.

The Sun came up upon the left,
Out of the sea came he!
And he shone bright, and on the right
Went down into the sea.

Higher and higher every day,
Till over the mast at noon—"   30
The Wedding-Guest here beat his breast,
For he heard the loud bassoon.

The Wedding-
Guest heareth the
bridal music;
but the Mariner
continueth
his tale.

The bride hath paced into the hall,
Red as a rose is she;
Nodding their heads before her goes
The merry minstrelsy.

The Wedding-Guest he beat his breast,
Yet he cannot choose but hear;
And thus spake on that ancient man,
The bright-eyed Mariner.   40

The ship driven
by a storm toward
the south pole.

"And now the STORM-BLAST came, and
     he
Was tyrannous and strong:
He struck with his o'ertaking wings,
And chased us south along.

With sloping masts and dipping prow,
As who pursued with yell and blow
Still treads the shadow of his foe,
And forward bends his head,
The ship drove fast, loud roared the
     blast,
And southward aye we fled.   50

And now there came both mist and
     snow,
And it grew wondrous cold:
And ice, mast-high, came floating by,
As green as emerald.

The land of ice,
and of fearful
sounds where
no living thing
was to be seen.

And through the drifts the snowy clifts
Did send a dismal sheen:
Nor shapes of men nor beasts we ken—
The ice was all between.

The ice was here, the ice was there,
The ice was all around: 60

It cracked and growled, and roared and
    howled,
Like noises in a swound!

Till a great
sea-bird, called
the Albatross,
came through the
snow-fog, and
was received with
great joy and
hospitality.

At length did cross an Albatross,
Thorough the fog it came;
As if it had been a Christian soul,
We hailed it in God's name.

It ate the food it ne'er had eat,
And round and round it flew.
The ice did split with a thunder-fit;
The helmsman steered us through!   70

And lo! the
Albatross proveth
a bird of good
omen, and
followeth the
ship as it
returned
northward
through fog
and floating ice.

And a good south wind sprung up be-
    hind;
The Albatross did follow,
And every day, for food or play,
Came to the mariner's hollo!

In mist or cloud, on mast or shroud,
It perched for vespers nine;
Whiles all the night, through fog-smoke
    white,
Glimmered the white Moon-shine."

The ancient
Mariner
inhospitably
killeth the
pious bird of
good omen.

"God save thee, ancient Mariner!
From the fiends, that plague the
    thus!—   8
Why look'st thou so?"—With my cross
    bow
I shot the ALBATROSS.

PART II

The Sun now rose upon the right:
Out of the sea came he,
Still hid in mist, and on the left
Went down into the sea.

And the good south wind still blew b
    hind,

But no sweet bird did follow,
Nor any day for food or play
Came to the mariners' hollo! 90

His shipmates
cry out against
the ancient
Mariner, for
killing the bird
of good luck.

And I had done a hellish thing,
And it would work 'em woe:
For all averred, I had killed the bird
That made the breeze to blow.
Ah wretch! said they, the bird to slay,
That made the breeze to blow!

But when the
fog cleared off,
they justify the
same, and thus
make themselves
accomplices in
the crime.

Nor dim nor red, like God's own head,
The glorious Sun uprist:
Then all averred, I had killed the bird
That brought the fog and mist. 100
'Twas right, said they, such birds to
    slay,
That bring the fog and mist.

The fair breeze
continues; the
ship enters the
Pacific Ocean,
and sails
northward, even
till it reaches
the Line.

The fair breeze blew, the white foam
    flew,
The furrow followed free;
We were the first that ever burst
Into that silent sea.

Down dropt the breeze, the sails dropt
    down,
'Twas sad as sad could be;
And we did speak only to break
The silence of the sea! 110

The ship hath
been suddenly
becalmed.

All in a hot and copper sky,
The bloody Sun, at noon,
Right up above the mast did stand,
No bigger than the Moon.

Day after day, day after day,
We stuck, nor breath nor motion;
As idle as a painted ship
Upon a painted ocean.

Water, water, every where,

And the Albatross
begins to be
avenged.

And all the boards did shrink;   120
Water, water, every where,
Nor any drop to drink.

The very deep did rot: O Christ!
That ever this should be!
Yea, slimy things did crawl with legs
Upon the slimy sea.

About, about, in reel and rout
The death-fires danced at night;
The water, like a witch's oils,
Burnt green, and blue and white.   130

A Spirit had
followed them;
one of the
invisible
inhabitants of
this planet, neither departed souls nor angels; concerning whom the
learned Jew, Josephus, and the Platonic Constantinopolitan, Michael
Psellus, may be consulted. They are very numerous, and there is
no climate or element without one or more.

And some in dreams assuréd were
Of the Spirit that plagued us so;
Nine fathom deep he had followed us
From the land of mist and snow.

And every tongue, through utter drought
Was withered at the root;
We could not speak, no more than if
We had been choked with soot.

The shipmates,
in their sore
distress, would
fain throw the
whole guilt on the
ancient Mariner:
in sign whereof they hang the dead sea-bird round his neck.

Ah! well a-day! what evil looks
Had I from old and young!   140
Instead of the cross, the Albatross
About my neck was hung.

PART III

There passed a weary time. Each throat
Was parched, and glazed each eye.
A weary time! a weary time!
How glazed each weary eye,

The ancient
Mariner
beholdeth a sign
in the element
afar off.

When looking westward, I beheld
A something in the sky.

At first it seemed a little speck,
And then it seemed a mist;   150
It moved and moved, and took at last
A certain shape, I wist.

A speck, a mist, a shape, I wist!
And still it neared and neared:
As if it dodged a water-sprite,
It plunged and tacked and veered.

At its nearer
approach, it
seemeth him to
be a ship; and
at a dear ransom
he freeth his
speech from the
bonds of thirst.

With throats unslaked, with black lips
    baked,
We could nor laugh nor wail;
Through utter drought all dumb we
    stood!
I bit my arm, I sucked the blood,   160
And cried, A sail! a sail!

With throats unslaked, with black lips
    baked,
Agape they heard me call:
Gramercy! they for joy did grin,
And all at once their breath drew in,
As they were drinking all.

A flash of joy;

And horror
follows. For can
it be a ship that
comes onward
without wind
or tide?

See! see! (I cried) she tacks no more!
Hither to work us weal;
Without a breeze, without a tide,
She steadies with upright keel!   170

The western wave was all a-flame.
The day was well nigh done!
Almost upon the western wave
Rested the broad bright Sun;
When that strange shape drove suddenly
Betwixt us and the Sun.

It seemeth him
but the skeleton
of a ship.

And straight the Sun was flecked with
    bars,

(Heaven's Mother send us grace!)
As if through a dungeon-grate he peered
With broad and burning face.   180

And its ribs are
seen as bars
on the face of the
setting Sun.

Alas! (thought I, and my heart beat
        loud)
How fast she nears and nears!
Are those *her* sails that glance in
        the Sun,
Like restless gossameres?

The Spectre-
Woman
and her
Deathmate,
and no other on
board the
skeleton ship.

Are those *her* ribs through which the Sun
Did peer, as through a grate?
And is that Woman all her crew?
Is that a DEATH? and are there two?
Is DEATH that woman's mate?

Like vessel,
like crew!

Her lips were red, *her* looks were free,
Her locks were yellow as gold: 191
Her skin was as white as leprosy,

Death and
Life-in-Death
have diced for the
ship's crew, and
she (the latter)
winneth the
ancient Mariner.

The Night-mare LIFE-IN-DEATH was she,
Who thicks man's blood with cold.

The naked hulk alongside came,
And the twain were casting dice;
"The game is done! I've won! I've won!
Quoth she, and whistles thrice.

No twilight
within the courts
of the Sun.

The Sun's rim dips; the stars rush out:
At one stride comes the dark;   20
With far-heard whisper, o'er the sea,
Off shot the spectre-bark.

At the rising of
the Moon,

We listened and looked sideways up!
Fear at my heart, as at a cup,
My life-blood seemed to sip!
The stars were dim, and thick the night,
The steersman's face by his lamp
        gleamed white;
From the sails the dew did drip—
Till clomb above the eastern bar

The hornéd Moon, with one bright star
Within the nether tip.   211

One after another,

One after one, by the star-dogged Moon,
Too quick for groan or sigh,
Each turned his face with a ghastly
        pang,
And cursed me with his eye.

His shipmates
drop down dead.

Four times fifty living men,
(And I heard nor sigh nor groan)
With heavy thump, a lifeless lump,
They dropped down one by one.

But Life-in-Death
begins her work
on the ancient
Mariner.

The souls did from their bodies fly,—
They fled to bliss or woe!   221
And every soul, it passed me by,
Like the whizz of my cross-bow!

PART IV

The Wedding-
Guest feareth
that a Spirit is
talking to him;

"I fear thee, ancient Mariner!
I fear thy skinny hand!
And thou art long, and lank, and brown,
As is the ribbed sea-sand.*

I fear thee and thy glittering eye,
And thy skinny hand, so brown."—

But the ancient
Mariner assureth
him of his
bodily life, and
proceedeth to
relate his
horrible penance.

Fear not, fear not, thou Wedding-Guest!
This body dropt not down.   231

Alone, alone, all, all alone,
Alone on a wide wide sea!
And never a saint took pity on
My soul in agony.

He despiseth the
creatures of
the calm,

The many men, so beautiful!
And they all dead did lie:
And a thousand thousand slimy things
Lived on; and so did I.

I looked upon the rotting sea,   240

[The Rime of the Ancient Mariner]   49

And drew my eyes away;
I looked upon the rotting deck,
And there the dead men lay.

And envieth that *they* should live, and so many lie dead.

And drew my eyes away;
I looked upon the rotting deck,
And there the dead men lay.

I looked to heaven, and tried to pray;
But or ever a prayer had gusht,
A wicked whisper came, and made
My heart as dry as dust.

I closed my lids, and kept them close,
And the balls like pulses beat;
For the sky and the sea, and the sea and
    the sky   250
Lay like a load on my weary eye,
And the dead were at my feet.

But the curse liveth for him in the eye of the dead men.

The cold sweat melted from their limbs,
Nor rot nor reek did they:
The look with which they looked on me
Had never passed away.

An orphan's curse would drag to hell
A spirit from on high;
But oh! more horrible than that
Is the curse in a dead man's eye!   260
Seven days, seven nights, I saw that
    curse,
And yet I could not die.

In his loneliness and fixedness he yearneth towards the journeying Moon, and the stars that still sojourn, yet still move onward; and every where the blue sky belongs to them,

The moving Moon went up the sky,
And no where did abide:
Softly she was going up,
And a star or two beside—

Her beams bemocked the sultry main,
Like April hoar-frost spread;
But where the ship's huge shadow lay,
The charméd water burnt alway   270

and is their appointed rest, and their native country and their own natural homes, which they enter unannounced, as lords that are certainly expected and yet there is a silent joy at their arrival.

A still and awful red.

By the light of
the Moon he
beholdeth God's
creatures of the
great calm.

Beyond the shadow of the ship,
I watched the water-snakes:
They moved in tracks of shining white,
And when they reared, the elfish light
Fell off in hoary flakes.

Within the shadow of the ship
I watched their rich attire:
Blue, glossy green, and velvet black,
They coiled and swam; and every track
Was a flash of golden fire.   281

Their beauty and
their happiness.

O happy living things! no tongue
Their beauty might declare:
A spring of love gushed from my heart,
And I blessed them unaware:

He blesseth them
in his heart.

Sure my kind saint took pity on me,
And I blessed them unaware.

The spell begins
to break.

The self-same moment I could pray;
And from my neck so free
The Albatross fell off, and sank   290
Like lead into the sea.

PART V

Oh sleep! it is a gentle thing,
Beloved from pole to pole!
To Mary Queen the praise be given!
She sent the gentle sleep from Heaven,
That slid into my soul.

By the grace of
the holy Mother,
the ancient
Mariner is
refreshed
with rain.

The silly buckets on the deck,
That had so long remained,
I dreamt that they were filled with dew;
And when I awoke, it rained.   300

My lips were wet, my throat was cold,
My garments all were dank;

Sure I had drunken in my dreams,
And still my body drank.

I moved, and could not feel my limbs:
I was so light—almost
I thought that I had died in sleep,
And was a blessèd ghost.

He heareth
sounds and seeth
strange sights
and commotions
in the sky and
the element.
And soon I heard a roaring wind:
It did not come anear;   310
But with its sound it shook the sails,
That were so thin and sere.

The upper air burst into life!
And a hundred fire-flags sheen,
To and fro they were hurried about!
And to and fro, and in and out,
The wan stars danced between.

And the coming wind did roar more
        loud,
And the sails did sigh like sedge;
And the rain poured down from on
        black cloud;   32
The Moon was at its edge.

The thick black cloud was cleft, and sti
The Moon was at its side:
Like waters shot from some high crag
The lightning fell with never a jag,
A river steep and wide.

The bodies of the
ship's crew are
inspired and the
ship moves on;
The loud wind never reached the ship,
Yet now the ship moved on!
Beneath the lightning and the Moon
The dead men gave a groan.   330

They groaned, they stirred, they all up-
        rose,
Nor spake, nor moved their eyes;
It had been strange, even in a dream,
To have seen those dead men rise.

The helmsman steered, the ship moved
on;
Yet never a breeze up-blew;
The mariners all 'gan work the ropes,
Where they were wont to do;
They raised their limbs like lifeless
tools—
We were a ghastly crew.   340

The body of my brother's son
Stood by me, knee to knee:
The body and I pulled at one rope,
But he said nought to me.

But not by the
souls of the men,
nor by dæmons
of earth or
middle air, but
by a blessed
troop of angelic
spirits, sent down
by the invocation
of the
guardian saint.
"I fear thee, ancient Mariner!"
Be calm, thou Wedding-Guest!
'Twas not those souls that fled in pain,
Which to their corses came again,
But a troop of spirits blest:

For when it dawned—they dropped their
arms,   350
And clustered round the mast;
Sweet sounds rose slowly through their
mouths,
And from their bodies passed.

Around, around, flew each sweet sound,
Then darted to the Sun;
Slowly the sounds came back again,
Now mixed, now one by one.

Sometimes a-dropping from the sky
I heard the sky-lark sing;
Sometimes all little birds that are,   360
How they seemed to fill the sea and air
With their sweet jargoning!

And now 'twas like all instruments,
Now like a lonely flute;
And now it is an angel's song,
That makes the heavens be mute.

It ceased; yet still the sails made on
A pleasant noise till noon,
A noise like of a hidden brook
In the leafy month of June,   370
That to the sleeping woods all night
Singeth a quiet tune.

Till noon we quietly sailed on,
Yet never a breeze did breathe:
Slowly and smoothly went the ship,
Moved onward from beneath.

The lonesome Spirit from the south-pole carries on the ship as far as the Line, in obedience to the angelic troop, but still requireth vengeance.

Under the keel nine fathom deep,
From the land of mist and snow,
The spirit slid: and it was he
That made the ship to go.   380
The sails at noon left off their tune,
And the ship stood still also.

The Sun, right up above the mast,
Had fixed her to the ocean:
But in a minute she 'gan stir,
With a short uneasy motion—
Backwards and forwards half her length
With a short uneasy motion.

Then like a pawing horse let go,
She made a sudden bound: 390
It flung the blood into my head,
And I fell down in a swound.

The Polar Spirit's fellow-daemons, the invisible inhabitants of the element, take part in his wrong; and two of them relate, one to the other, that penance long and heavy for the ancient Mariner hath

How long in that same fit I lay,
I have not to declare;
But ere my living life returned,
I heard and in my soul discerned
Two voices in the air.

"Is it he?" quoth one, "Is this the man?
By him who died on cross,
With his cruel bow he laid full low   400
The harmless Albatross.

been accorded to
the Polar Spirit,
who returneth
southward.

The spirit who bideth by himself
In the land of mist and snow,
He loved the bird that loved the man
Who shot him with his bow."

The other was a softer voice,
As soft as honey-dew:
Quoth he, "The man hath penance done,
And penance more will do."

PART VI

FIRST VOICE

"But tell me, tell me! speak again,   410
Thy soft response renewing—
What makes that ship drive / so fast?
What is the ocean doing?"

SECOND VOICE

"Still as a slave before h   d,
The ocean hath no blas'
His great bright eye m   ilently
Up to the Moon is ca

If he may know wh   way to go;
For she guides hin   ooth or grim.
See, brother, see!   v graciously   420
She looketh dov   n him."

FIRST VOI

The Mariner hath
been cast into a
trance; for the
angelic power
causeth the
vessel to drive
northward faster
than human life
could endure.

"But why dr   s on that ship so fast,
Without or   ve or wind?"

SECO   VOICE

"The air   s cut away before,
And cl   es from behind.

Fly,   other, fly! more high, more high!
Or   shall be belated:

For slow and slow that ship will go,
When the Mariner's trance is abated."

I woke, and we were sailing on   430
As in a gentle weather:
'Twas night, calm night, the moon was
          high;
The dead men stood together.

All stood together on the deck,
For a charnel-dungeon fitter:
All fixed on me their stony eyes,
That in the Moon did glitter.

The pang, the curse, with which they
          died,
Had never passed away:
I could not draw my eyes from theirs,
Nor turn them up to pray.   441

And now this spell was snapt: once
          more
I viewed the ocean green,
And looked far forth, yet little saw
Of what had else been seen—

Like one, that on a lonesome road
Doth walk in fear and dread,
And having once turned round walks on
And turns no more his head;
Because he knows, a frightful fiend   450
Doth close behind him tread.

But soon there breathed a wind on me,
Nor sound nor motion made:
Its path was not upon the sea,
In ripple or in shade.

It raised my hair, it fanned my cheek
Like a meadow-gale of spring—
It mingled strangely with my fears,
Yet it felt like a welcoming.

Swiftly, swiftly flew the ship,   460
Yet she sailed softly too:
Sweetly, sweetly blew the breeze—
On me alone it blew.

And the ancient
Mariner
beholdeth his
native country.

Oh! dream of joy! is this indeed
The light-house top I see?
Is this the hill? is this the kirk?
Is this mine own countree?

We drifted o'er the harbour-bar,
And I with sobs did pray—
O let me be awake, my God!   47
Or let me sleep alway.

The harbour-bay was clear as glass,
So smoothly it was strewn!
And on the bay the moonlight lay,
And the shadow of the Moon.

The rock shone bright, the kirk   ss,
That stands above the rock:
The moonlight steeped in sile   s
The steady weathercock.

And the bay was white with   t light,
Till rising from the same,   481

The angelic
spirits leave the
dead bodies,

Full many shapes, that sh   s were,
In crimson colours cam

A little distance from   prow
Those crimson shado   were:

And appear in
their own forms
of light.

I turned my eyes up   the deck—
Oh, Christ! what sa   I there!

Each corse lay fla feless and flat,
And, by the holy   d!
A man all light,   raph-man,   490
On every corse   re stood.

This seraph-b d, each waved his hand:
It was a heavenly sight!

They stood as signals to the land,
Each one a lovely light;

This seraph-band, each waved his hand,
No voice did they impart—
No voice; but oh! the silence sank
Like music on my heart.

But soon I heard the dash of oars,　　500
I heard the Pilot's cheer;
My head was turned perforce away
And I saw a boat appear.

The Pilot and the Pilot's boy,
I heard them coming fast:
Dear Lord in Heaven! it was a joy
The dead men could not blast.

I saw a third—I heard his voice:
It is the Hermit good!
He singeth loud his godly hymns　　510
That he makes in the wood.
He'll shrieve my soul, he'll wash away
The Albatross's blood.

PART VII

The Hermit
of the Wood,

This Hermit good lives in that wood
Which slopes down to the sea.
How loudly his sweet voice he rears!
He loves to talk with marineres
That come from a far countree.

He kneels at morn, and noon, and eve—
He hath a cushion plump:　　520
It is the moss that wholly hides
The rotted old oak-stump.

The skiff-boat neared: I heard them talk,
"Why, this is strange, I trow!
Where are those lights so many and fair,
That signal made but now?"

"Strange, by my faith!" the Hermit
    said—
"And they answered not our cheer!
The planks looked warped! and see those
    sails,
How thin they are and sere!   530
I never saw aught like to them,
    Unless perchance it were

Brown skeletons of leaves that lag
    My forest-brook along;
When the ivy-tod is heavy with snow,
And the owlet whoops to the wolf below,
    That eats the she-wolf's young."

"Dear Lord! it hath a fiendish look—
    (The Pilot made reply)
I am a-feared"—"Push on, push on!"
    Said the Hermit cheerily.   541

The boat came closer to the ship,
    But I nor spake nor stirred;
The boat came close beneath the ship,
    And straight a sound was heard.

Under the water it rumbled on,
    Still louder and more dread:
It reached the ship, it split the bay;
    The ship went down like lead.

The ancient
Mariner is
saved in the
Pilot's boat.

Stunned by that loud and dreadful
    sound,   550
Which sky and ocean smote,
Like one that hath been seven days
    drowned
My body lay afloat;
But swift as dreams, myself I found
    Within the Pilot's boat.

Upon the whirl, where sank the ship,
    The boat spun round and round;

And all was still, save that the hill
Was telling of the sound.

I moved my lips—the Pilot shrieked   560
And fell down in a fit;
The holy Hermit raised his eyes,
And prayed where he did sit.

I took the oars: the Pilot's boy,
Who now doth crazy go,
Laughed loud and long, and all the
        while
His eyes went to and fro.
"Ha! ha!" quoth he, "full plain I see,
The Devil knows how to row."

And now, all in my own countree,   570
I stood on the firm land!
The Hermit stepped forth from the boat,
And scarcely he could stand.

"O shrieve me, shrieve me, holy man!"
The Hermit crossed his brow.
"Say quick," quoth he, "I bid thee say—
What manner of man art thou?"

Forthwith this frame of mine was
        wrenched
With a woful agony,
Which forced me to begin my tale;   580
And then it left me free.

Since then, at an uncertain hour,
That agony returns:
And till my ghastly tale is told,
This heart within me burns.

I pass, like night, from land to land;
I have strange power of speech;
That moment that his face I see,
I know the man that must hear me:
To him my tale I teach.   590

[*The Rime of the Ancient Mariner*]   60

What loud uproar bursts from that door!
The wedding-guests are there:
But in the garden-bower the bride
And bride-maids singing are:
And hark the little vesper bell,
Which biddeth me to prayer!

O Wedding-Guest! this soul hath been
Alone on a wide wide sea:
So lonely 'twas, that God himself
Scarce seeméd there to be.   600

O sweeter than the marriage-feast,
'Tis sweeter far to me,
To walk together to the kirk
With a goodly company!—

To walk together to the kirk,
And all together pray,
While each to his great Father bends,
Old men, and babes, and loving friends
And youths and maidens gay!

And to teach,
by his own
example, love
and reverence to
all things that
God made
and loveth.

Farewell, farewell! but this I tell   610
To thee, thou Wedding-Guest!
He prayeth well, who loveth well
Both man and bird and beast.

He prayeth best, who loveth best
All things both great and small;
For the dear God who loveth us,
He made and loveth all.

The Mariner, whose eye is bright,
Whose beard with age is hoar,   619
Is gone: and now the Wedding-Guest
Turned from the bridegroom's door.

He went like one that hath been stunned,
And is of sense forlorn:
A sadder and a wiser man,
He rose the morrow morn.

Christabel

PREFACE

The first part of the following poem was written in the year 1797, at Stowey, in the county of Somerset. The second part, after my return from Germany, in the year 1800, at Keswick, Cumberland. It is probable that if the poem had been finished at either of the former periods, or if even the first and second part had been published in the year 1800, the impression of its originality would have been much greater than I dare at present expect. But for this I have only my own indolence to blame. The dates are mentioned for the exclusive purpose of precluding charges of plagiarism or servile imitation from myself. For there is amongst us a set of critics, who seem to hold, that every possible thought and image is traditional; who have no notion that there are such things as fountains in the world, small as well as great; and who would therefore charitably derive every rill they behold flowing, from a perforation made in some other man's tank. I am confident, however, that as far as the present poem is concerned, the celebrated poets whose writings I might be suspected of having imitated, either in particular passages, or in the tone and the spirit of the whole, would be among the first to vindicate me from the charge, and who, on any striking coincidence, would permit me to address them in this doggerel version of two monkish Latin hexameters.

'Tis mine and it is likewise yours;
But an' if this will not do,
Let it be mine, good friend! for I
Am the poorer of the two.

I have only to add that the metre of Christabel is not, properly speaking, irregular, though it may seem so from its being founded on a new principle: namely, that of counting in each line the accents, not the syllables. Though the latter may vary from seven to twelve, yet in

each line the accents will be found to be only four. Never-
theless, this occasional variation in number of syllables is
not introduced wantonly, or for the mere ends of conven-
ience, but in correspondence with some transition in the
nature of the imagery or passion.

PART I

'Tis the middle of night by the castle clock,
And the owls have awakened the crowing cock;
Tu—whit!——Tu—whoo!
And hark, again! the crowing cock,
How drowsily it crew.

Sir Leoline, the Baron rich,
Hath a toothless mastiff bitch;
From her kennel beneath the rock
She maketh answer to the clock,
Four for the quarters, and twelve for the hour;   10
Ever and aye, by shine and shower,
Sixteen short howls, not over loud;
Some say, she sees my lady's shroud.

Is the night chilly and dark?
The night is chilly, but not dark.
The thin gray cloud is spread on high,
It covers but not hides the sky.
The moon is behind, and at the full;
And yet she looks both small and dull.
The night is chill, the cloud is gray: 20
'Tis a month before the month of May,
And the Spring comes slowly up this way.

The lovely lady, Christabel,
Whom her father loves so well,
What makes her in the wood so late,
A furlong from the castle gate?
She had dreams all yesternight
Of her own bethrothéd knight;

And she in the midnight wood will pray
For the weal of her lover that's far away.   30

She stole along, she nothing spoke,
The sighs she heaved were soft and low,
And naught was green upon the oak
But moss and rarest mistletoe:
She kneels beneath the huge oak tree,
And in silence prayeth she.

The lady sprang up suddenly,
The lovely lady, Christabel!
It moaned as near, as near can be,
But what it is she cannot tell.—   40
On the other side it seems to be,
Of the huge, broad-breasted, old oak tree.

The night is chill; the forest bare;
Is it the wind that moaneth bleak?
There is not wind enough in the air
To move away the ringlet curl
From the lovely lady's cheek—
There is not wind enough to twirl
The one red leaf, the last of its clan,
That dances as often as dance it can,   50
Hanging so light, and hanging so high,
On the topmost twig that looks up at the sky.

Hush, beating heart of Christabel!
Jesu, Maria, shield her well!
She folded her arms beneath her cloak,
And stole to the other side of the oak.
        What sees she there?

There she sees a damsel bright,
Drest in a silken robe of white,
That shadowy in the moonlight shone: 60
The neck that made that white robe wan,
Her stately neck, and arms were bare;

Her blue-veined feet unsandal'd were,
And wildly glittered here and there
The gems entangled in her hair.
I guess, 'twas frightful there to see
A lady so richly clad as she—
Beautiful exceedingly!

Mary mother, save me now!
(Said Christabel,) And who art thou?   70

The lady strange made answer meet,
And her voice was faint and sweet:—
Have pity on my sore distress,
I scarce can speak for weariness:
Stretch forth thy hand, and have no fear!
Said Christabel, How camest thou here?
And the lady, whose voice was faint and sweet,
Did thus pursue her answer meet:—

My sire is of a noble line,
And my name is Geraldine: 80
Five warriors seized me yestermorn,
Me, even me, a maid forlorn:
They choked my cries with force and fright,
And tied me on a palfrey white.
The palfrey was as fleet as wind,
And they rode furiously behind.
They spurred amain, their steeds were white:
And once we crossed the shade of night.
As sure as Heaven shall rescue me,
I have no thought what men they be;   90
Nor do I know how long it is
(For I have lain entranced I wis)
Since one, the tallest of the five,
Took me from the palfrey's back,
A weary woman, scarce alive.
Some muttered words his comrades spoke:
He placed me underneath this oak;
He swore they would return with haste;

Whither they went I cannot tell—
I thought I heard, some minutes past,   100
Sounds as of a castle bell.
Stretch forth thy hand (thus ended she),
And help a wretched maid to flee.

Then Christabel stretched forth her hand,
And comforted fair Geraldine:
O well, bright dame! may you command
The service of Sir Leoline;
And gladly our stout chivalry
Will he send forth and friends withal
To guide and guard you safe and free   110
Home to your noble father's hall.

She rose: and forth with steps they passed
That strove to be, and were not, fast.
Her gracious stars the lady blest,
And thus spake on sweet Christabel:
All our household are at rest,
The hall as silent as the cell;
Sir Leoline is weak in health,
And may not well awakened be,
But we will move as if in stealth,   120
And I beseech your courtesy,
This night, to share your couch with me.

They crossed the moat, and Christabel
Took the key that fitted well;
A little door she opened straight,
All in the middle of the gate;
The gate that was ironed within and without,
Where an army in battle array had marched out.
The lady sank, belike through pain,
And Christabel with might and main   130
Lifted her up, a weary weight,
Over the threshold of the gate: *
Then the lady rose again,

And moved, as she were not in pain.

So free from danger, free from fear,
They crossed the court: right glad they were.
And Christabel devoutly cried
To the lady by her side,
Praise we the Virgin all divine
Who hath rescued thee from thy distress!   140
Alas, alas! said Geraldine,
I cannot speak for weariness.
So free from danger, free from fear,
They crossed the court: right glad they were.

Outside her kennel, the mastiff old
Lay fast asleep, in moonshine cold.
The mastiff old did not awake,
Yet she an angry moan did make!
And what can ail the mastiff bitch?
Never till now she uttered yell   150
Beneath the eye of Christabel.
Perhaps it is the owlet's scritch:
For what can ail the mastiff bitch?

They passed the hall, that echoes still,
Pass as lightly as you will!
The brands were flat, the brands were dying,
Amid their own white ashes lying
But when the lady passed, there came
A tongue of light, a fit of flame;
And Christabel saw the lady's eye,   160
And nothing else saw she thereby,
Save the boss of the shield of Sir Leoline tall,
Which hung in a murky old niche in the wall.
O softly tread, said Christabel,
My father seldom sleepeth well.

Sweet Christabel her feet doth bare,
And jealous of the listening air

They steal their way from stair to stair,
Now in glimmer, and now in gloom,
And now they pass the Baron's room,   170
As still as death, with stifled breath!
And now have reached her chamber door;
And now doth Geraldine press down
The rushes of the chamber floor.

The moon shines dim in the open air,
And not a moonbeam enters here.
But they without its light can see
The chamber carved so curiously,
Carved with figures strange and sweet,
All made out of the carver's brain,   180
For a lady's chamber meet:
The lamp with twofold silver chain
Is fastened to an angel's feet.

The silver lamp burns dead and dim;
But Christabel the lamp will trim.
She trimmed the lamp, and made it bright,
And left it swinging to and fro,
While Geraldine, in wretched plight,
Sank down upon the floor below.

O weary lady, Geraldine,   190
I pray you, drink this cordial wine!
It is a wine of virtuous powers;
My mother made it of wild flowers.

And will your mother pity me,
Who am a maiden most forlorn?
Christabel answered—Woe is me!
She died the hour that I was born.
I have heard the grey-haired friar tell
How on her death-bed she did say,
That she should hear the castle-bell   200
Strike twelve upon my wedding-day.
O mother dear! that thou wert here!

I would, said Geraldine, she were!

But soon with altered voice, said she—
"Off, wandering mother! Peak and pine!
I have power to bid thee flee."
Alas! what ails poor Geraldine?
Why stares she with unsettled eye?
Can she the bodiless dead espy?
And why with hollow voice cries she,   210
"Off, woman, off! this hour is mine—
Though thou her guardian spirit be,
Off, woman, off! 'tis given to me."

Then Christabel knelt by the lady's side,
And raised to heaven her eyes so blue—
Alas! said she, this ghastly ride—
Dear lady! it hath wildered you!
The lady wiped her moist cold brow,
And faintly said, " 'tis over now!"

Again the wild-flower wine she drank: 220
Her fair large eyes 'gan glitter bright,
And from the floor whereon she sank,
The lofty lady stood upright:
She was most beautiful to see,
Like a lady of a far countrée.

And thus the lofty lady spake—
"All they who live in the upper sky,
Do love you, holy Christabel!
And you love them, and for their sake
And for the good which me befel,   230
Even I in my degree will try,
Fair maiden, to requite you well.
But now unrobe yourself; for I
Must pray, ere yet in bed I lie."

Quoth Christabel, So let it be!
And as the lady bade, did she.

Her gentle limbs did she undress,
And lay down in her loveliness.

But through her brain of weal and woe
So many thoughts moved to and fro,   240
That vain it were her lids to close;
So half-way from the bed she rose,
And on her elbow did recline
To look at the lady Geraldine.

Beneath the lamp the lady bowed,
And slowly rolled her eyes around;
Then drawing in her breath aloud,
Like one that shuddered, she unbound
The cincture from beneath her breast:
Her silken robe, and inner vest,   250
Dropt to her feet, and full in view,
Behold! her bosom and half her side——
A sight to dream of, not to tell!
O shield her! shield sweet Christabel!

Yet Geraldine nor speaks nor stirs;
Ah! what a stricken look was hers!
Deep from within she seems half-way
To lift some weight with sick assay,
And eyes the maid and seeks delay;
Then suddenly, as one defied,   260
Collects herself in scorn and pride,
And lay down by the Maiden's side!—
And in her arms the maid she took,
              Ah wel-a-day!
And with low voice and doleful look
These words did say:
"In the touch of this bosom there worketh a spell,
Which is lord of thy utterance, Christabel!
Thou knowest to-night, and wilt know to-morrow,
This mark of my shame, this seal of my sorrow;   270
          But vainly thou warrest,
             For this is alone in

Thy power to declare,
        That in the dim forest
        Thou heard'st a low moaning,
And found'st a bright lady, surpassingly fair;
And didst bring her home with thee in love and in char-
        ity,
To shield her and shelter her from the damp air."

THE CONCLUSION TO PART I

It was a lovely sight to see
The lady Christabel, when she   280
Was praying at the old oak tree.
        Amid the jaggéd shadows
        Of mossy leafless boughs,
        Kneeling in the moonlight,
        To make her gentle vows;
Her slender palms together prest,
Heaving sometimes on her breast;
Her face resigned to bliss or bale—
Her face, oh call it fair not pale,
And both blue eyes more bright than clear,   290
Each about to have a tear.

With open eyes (ah woe is me!)
Asleep, and dreaming fearfully,
Fearfully dreaming, yet, I wis,
Dreaming that alone, which is—
O sorrow and shame! Can this be she,
The lady, who knelt at the old oak tree?
And lo! the worker of these harms,
That holds the maiden in her arms,
Seems to slumber still and mild,   300
As a mother with her child.

A star hath set, a star hath risen,
O Geraldine! since arms of thine
Have been the lovely lady's prison.
O Geraldine! one hour was thine—

Thou'st had thy will! By tairn and rill,
The night-birds all that hour were still.
But now they are jubilant anew,
From cliff and tower, tu—whoo! tu—whoo!
Tu—whoo! tu—whoo! from wood and fell!   310

And see! the lady Christabel
Gathers herself from out her trance;
Her limbs relax, her countenance
Grows sad and soft; the smooth thin lids
Close o'er her eyes; and tears she sheds—
Large tears that leave the lashes bright!
And oft the while she seems to smile
As infants at a sudden light!

Yea, she doth smile, and she doth weep,
Like a youthful hermitess,   320
Beauteous in a wilderness,
Who, praying always, prays in sleep.
And, if she move unquietly,
Perchance, 'tis but the blood so free
Comes back and tingles in her feet.
No doubt, she hath a vision sweet.
What if her guardian spirit 'twere,
What if she knew her mother near?
But this she knows, in joys and woes,
That saints will aid if men will call: 330
For the blue sky bends over all!

PART II

Each matin bell, the Baron saith,
Knells us back to a world of death.
These words Sir Leoline first said,
When he rose and found his lady dead:
These words Sir Leoline will say
Many a morn to his dying day!

And hence the custom and law began

That still at dawn the sacristan,
Who duly pulls the heavy bell,   340
Five and forty beads must tell
Between each stroke—a warning knell,
Which not a soul can choose but hear
From Bratha Head to Wyndermere.

Saith Bracy the bard, So let it knell!
And let the drowsy sacristan
Still count as slowly as he can!
There is no lack of such, I ween,
As well fill up the space between.
In Langdale Pike and Witch's Lair,*   350
And Dungeon-ghyll so foully rent,*
With ropes of rock and bells of air
Three sinful sextons' ghosts are pent,
Who all give back, one after t'other,
The death-note to their living brother;
And oft too, by the knell offended,
Just as their one! two! three! is ended,
The devil mocks the doleful tale
With a merry peal from Borodale.

he air is still! through mist and cloud   360
hat merry peal comes ringing loud;
nd Geraldine shakes off her dread,
nd rises lightly from the bed;
uts on her silken vestments white,
And tricks her hair in lovely plight,*
And nothing doubting of her spell
Awakens the lady Christabel.
"Sleep you, sweet lady Christabel?
I trust that you have rested well."

And Christabel awoke and spied   370
The same who lay down by her side—
O rather say, the same whom she
Raised up beneath the old oak tree!
Nay, fairer yet! and yet more fair!

For she belike hath drunken deep
Of all the blessedness of sleep!
And while she spake, her looks, her air
Such gentle thankfulness declare,
That (so it seemed) her girded vests
Grew tight beneath her heaving breasts.   380
"Sure I have sinn'd!" said Christabel,
"Now heaven be praised if all be well!"
And in low faltering tones, yet sweet,
Did she the lofty lady greet
With such perplexity of mind
As dreams too lively leave behind.

So quickly she rose, and quickly arrayed
Her maiden limbs, and having prayed
That He, who on the cross did groan,
Might wash away her sins unknown,   390
She forthwith led fair Geraldine
To meet her sire, Sir Leoline.

The lovely maid and the lady tall
Are pacing both into the hall,
And pacing on through page and groom,
Enter the Baron's presence-room.

The Baron rose, and while he prest
His gentle daughter to his breast,
With cheerful wonder in his eyes
The lady Geraldine espies,   400
And gave such welcome to the same,
As might beseem so bright a dame!

But when he heard the lady's tale,
And when she told her father's name,
Why waxed Sir Leoline so pale,
Murmuring o'er the name again,
Lord Roland de Vaux of Tryermaine?

Alas! they had been friends in youth;*

But whispering tongues can poison truth;
And constancy lives in realms above;   410
And life is thorny; and youth is vain;
And to be wroth with one we love
Doth work like madness in the brain.
And thus it chanced, as I divine,
With Roland and Sir Leoline.
Each spake words of high disdain
And insult to his heart's best brother:
They parted—ne'er to meet again!
But never either found another
To free the hollow heart from paining—   420
They stood aloof, the scars remaining,
Like cliffs which had been rent asunder;
A dreary sea now flows between;—
But neither heat, nor frost, nor thunder,
Shall wholly do away, I ween,
The marks of that which once hath been.

Sir Leoline, a moment's space,
Stood gazing on the damsel's face:
And the youthful Lord of Tryermaine
Came back upon his heart again.   430

O then the Baron forgot his age,
His noble heart swelled high with rage;
He swore by the wounds in Jesu's side
He would proclaim it far and wide,
With trump and solemn heraldry,
That they, who thus had wronged the dame,
Were base as spotted infamy!
"And if they dare deny the same,
My herald shall appoint a week,
And let the recreant traitors seek   440
My tourney court—that there and then
I may dislodge their reptile souls
From the bodies and forms of men!"
He spake: his eye in lightning rolls!
For the lady was ruthlessly seized; and he kenned

In the beautiful lady the child of his friend!

And now the tears were on his face,
And fondly in his arms he took
Fair Geraldine, who met the embrace,
Prolonging it with joyous look.   450
Which when she viewed, a vision fell
Upon the soul of Christabel,
The vision of fear, the touch and pain!
She shrunk and shuddered, and saw again—
(Ah, woe is me! Was it for thee,
Thou gentle maid! such sights to see?)

Again she saw that bosom old,
Again she felt that bosom cold,
And drew in her breath with a hissing sound:
Whereat the Knight turned wildly round,   460
And nothing saw, but his own sweet maid
With eyes upraised, as one that prayed.

The touch, the sight, had passed away,
And in its stead that vision blest,
Which comforted her after-rest
While in the lady's arms she lay,
Had put a rapture in her breast,
And on her lips and o'er her eyes
Spread smiles like light!
                           With new surprise,
"What ails then my belovéd child?"   470
The Baron said—His daughter mild
Made answer, "All will yet be well!"
I ween, she had no power to tell
Aught else: so mighty was the spell.

Yet he, who saw this Geraldine,
Had deemed her sure a thing divine:
Such sorrow with such grace she blended,
As if she feared she had offended
Sweet Christabel, that gentle maid!

And with such lowly tones she prayed 480
She might be sent without delay
Home to her father's mansion.

                    "Nay!
Nay, by my soul!" said Leoline.
"Ho! Bracy the bard, the charge be thine!
Go thou, with music sweet and loud,
And take two steeds with trappings proud,
And take the youth whom thou lov'st best
To bear thy harp, and learn thy song,
And clothe you both in solemn vest,
And over the mountains haste along, 490
Lest wandering folk, that are abroad,
Detain you on the valley road.

"And when he has crossed the Irthing flood,
My merry bard! he hastes, he hastes
Up Knorren Moor, through Halegarth Wood,
And reaches soon that castle good
Which stands and threatens Scotland's wastes.

"Bard Bracy! bard Bracy! your horses are fleet,
Ye must ride up the hall, your music so sweet,
More loud than your horses' echoing feet! 500
And loud and loud to Lord Roland call,
Thy daughter is safe in Langdale hall!
Thy beautiful daughter is safe and free—
Sir Leoline greets thee thus through me!
He bids thee come without delay
With all thy numerous array
And take thy lovely daughter home:
And he will meet thee on the way
With all his numerous array
White with their panting palfreys' foam: 510
And, by mine honour! I will say,
That I repent me of the day
When I spake words of fierce disdain
To Roland de Vaux of Tryermaine!—
—For since that evil hour hath flown,

Many a summer's sun hath shone;
Yet ne'er found I a friend again
Like Roland de Vaux of Tryermaine."

The lady fell, and clasped his knees,
Her face upraised, her eyes o'erflowing;   520
And Bracy replied, with faltering voice,
His gracious Hail on all bestowing!—
"Thy words, thou sire of Christabel,
Are sweeter than my harp can tell;
Yet might I gain a boon of thee,
This day my journey should not be,
So strange a dream hath come to me,
That I had vowed with music loud
To clear yon wood from thing unblest,
Warned by a vision in my rest!   530
For in my sleep I saw that dove,
That gentle bird, whom thou dost love,
And call'st by thy own daughter's name—
Sir Leoline! I saw the same
Fluttering, and uttering fearful moan,
Among the green herbs in the forest alone.
Which when I saw and when I heard,
I wonder'd what might ail the bird;
For nothing near it could I see,   539
Save the grass and green herbs underneath the old tree.

"And in my dream methought I went
earch out what might there be found;
what the sweet bird's trouble meant,
hus lay fluttering on the ground.
nd peered, and could descry
No ca   for her distressful cry;
But yet   her dear lady's sake
I stooped, methought, the dove to take,
When lo! I saw a bright green snake
Coiled around its wings and neck.   550
Green as the herbs on which it couched,
Close by the dove's its head it crouched;

And with the dove it heaves and stirs,
Swelling its neck as she swelled hers!
I woke; it was the midnight hour,
The clock was echoing in the tower;
But though my slumber was gone by,
This dream it would not pass away—
It seems to live upon my eye!
And thence I vowed this self-same day   560
With music strong and saintly song
To wander through the forest bare,
Lest aught unholy loiter there."

Thus Bracy said: the Baron, the while,
Half-listening heard him with a smile;
Then turned to Lady Geraldine,
His eyes made up of wonder and love;
And said in courtly accents fine,
"Sweet maid, Lord Roland's beauteous dove,
With arms more strong than harp or song,   570
Thy sire and I will crush the snake!"
He kissed her forehead as he spake,
And Geraldine in maiden wise
Casting down her large bright eyes,
With blushing cheek and courtesy fine
She turned her from Sir Leoline;
Softly gathering up her train,
That o'er her right arm fell again;
And folded her arms across her chest,
And couched her head upon her breast,   580
And looked askance at Christabel——
Jesu, Maria, shield her well!

A snake's small eye blinks dull and shy;
And the lady's eyes they shrunk in her head,
Each shrunk up to a serpent's eye,
And with somewhat of malice, and more of dread,
At Christabel she looked askance!—
One moment—and the sight was fled!
But Christabel in dizzy trance

Stumbling on the unsteady ground   590
Shuddered aloud, with a hissing sound;
And Geraldine again turned round,
And like a thing, that sought relief,
Full of wonder and full of grief,
She rolled her large bright eyes divine
Wildly on Sir Leoline.

The maid, alas! her thoughts are gone,
She nothing sees—no sight but one!
The maid, devoid of guile and sin,
I know not how, in fearful wise,   600
So deeply had she drunken in
That look, those shrunken serpent eyes,
That all her features were resigned
To this sole image in her mind:
And passively did imitate
That look of dull and treacherous hate!
And thus she stood, in dizzy trance,
Still picturing that look askance
With forced unconscious sympathy
Full before her father's view——   610
As far as such a look could be
In eyes so innocent and blue!

And when the trance was o'er, the maid
Paused awhile, and inly prayed:
Then falling at the Baron's feet,
"By my mother's soul do I entreat
That thou this woman send away!"
She said: and more she could not say:
For what she knew she could not tell,
O'er-mastered by the mighty spell.   620

Why is thy cheek so wan and wild,
Sir Leoline? Thy only child
Lies at thy feet, thy joy, thy pride,
So fair, so innocent, so mild;
The same, for whom thy lady died!

O by the pangs of her dear mother
Think thou no evil of thy child!
For her, and thee, and for no other,
She prayed the moment ere she died:
Prayed that the babe for whom she died,   630
Might prove her dear lord's joy and pride!
    That prayer her deadly pangs beguiled,
      Sir Leoline!
    And wouldst thou wrong thy only child,
      Her child and thine?

Within the Baron's heart and brain
If thoughts, like these, had any share,
They only swelled his rage and pain,
And did but work confusion there.
His heart was cleft with pain and rage,   640
His cheeks they quivered, his eyes were wild,
Dishonoured thus in his old age;
Dishonoured by his only child,
And all his hospitality
To the wronged daughter of his friend
By more than woman's jealousy
Brought thus to a disgraceful end—
He rolled his eye with stern regard
Upon the gentle minstrel bard,
And said in tones abrupt, austere—   650
"Why, Bracy! dost thou loiter here?
I bade thee hence!" The bard obeyed;
And turning from his own sweet maid,
The agéd knight, Sir Leoline,
Led forth the lady Geraldine!

THE CONCLUSION TO PART II

A little child, a limber elf,
Singing, dancing to itself,
A fairy thing with red round cheeks,
That always finds, and never seeks,
Makes such a vision to the sight   660

As fills a father's eyes with light;
And pleasures flow in so thick and fast
Upon his heart, that he at last
Must needs express his love's excess
With words of unmeant bitterness.
Perhaps 'tis pretty to force together
Thoughts so all unlike each other;
To mutter and mock a broken charm,
To dally with wrong that does no harm.
Perhaps 'tis tender too and pretty   670
At each wild word to feel within
A sweet recoil of love and pity.
And what, if in a world of sin
(O sorrow and shame should this be true!)
Such giddiness of heart and brain
Comes seldom save from rage and pain,
So talks as it's most used to do.

Frost at Midnight

The Frost performs its secret ministry,
Unhelped by any wind. The owlet's cry
Came loud—and hard, again! loud as before.
The inmates of my cottage, all at rest,
Have left me to that solitude, which suits
Abstruser musings: save that at my side
My cradled infant slumbers peacefully.
'Tis calm indeed! so calm, that it disturbs
And vexes meditation with its strange
And extreme silentness. Sea, hill, and wood,   10
This populous village! Sea, and hill, and wood,
With all the numberless goings-on of life,
Inaudible as dreams! the thin blue flame
Lies on my low-burnt fire, and quivers not;
Only that film, which fluttered on the grate,*
Still flutters there, the sole unquiet thing.
Methinks, its motion in this hush of nature
Gives it dim sympathies with me who live,

Making it a companionable form,
Whose puny flaps and freaks the idling Spirit   20
By its own moods interprets, every where
Echo or mirror seeking of itself,
And makes a toy of Thought.

                  But O! how oft,
How oft, at school, with most believing mind,
Presageful, have I gazed upon the bars,
To watch that fluttering *stranger!* and as oft
With unclosed lids, already had I dreamt
Of my sweet birth-place, and the old church-tower,
Whose bells, the poor man's only music, rang
From morn to evening, all the hot Fair-day,   30
So sweetly, that they stirred and haunted me
With a wild pleasure, falling on mine ear
Most like articulate sounds of things to come!
So gazed I, till the soothing things, I dreamt,
Lulled me to sleep, and sleep prolonged my dreams!
And so I brooded all the following morn,
Awed by the stern preceptor's face, mine eye
Fixed with mock study on my swimming book:
Save if the door half opened, and I snatched
A hasty glance, and still my heart leaped up,   40
For still I hoped to see the *stranger's* face,
Townsman, or aunt, or sister more beloved,
My play-mate when we both were clothed alike!

    Dear Babe, that sleepest cradled by my side,
Whose gentle breathings, heard in this deep calm,
Fill up the interspersèd vacancies
And momentary pauses of the thought!
My babe so beautiful! it thrills my heart
With tender gladness, thus to look at thee,
And think that thou shalt learn far other lore,   50
And in far other scenes! For I was reared
In the great city, pent 'mid cloisters dim,
And saw nought lovely but the sky and stars.
But *thou*, my babe! shalt wander like a breeze

By lakes and sandy shores, beneath the crags
Of ancient mountain, and beneath the clouds,
Which image in their bulk both lakes and shores
And mountain crags: so shalt thou see and hear
The lovely shapes and sounds intelligible
Of that eternal language, which thy God   60
Utters, who from eternity doth teach
Himself in all, and all things in himself.
Great universal Teacher! he shall mould
Thy spirit, and by giving make it ask.

Therefore all seasons shall be sweet to thee,
Whether the summer clothe the general earth
With greenness, or the redbreast sit and sing
Betwixt the tufts of snow on the bare branch
Of mossy apple-tree, while the nigh thatch
Smokes in the sun-thaw; whether the eave-drops fall   70
Heard only in the trances of the blast,
Or if the secret ministry of frost
Shall hang them up in silent icicles,
Quietly shining to the quiet Moon.

France: An Ode

I

Ye Clouds! that far above me float and pause,*
   Whose pathless march no mortal may controul!
  Ye Ocean-Waves! that, wheresoe'er ye roll,
Yield homage only to eternal laws!
Ye Woods! that listen to the night-birds singing,
   Midway the smooth and perilous slope reclined,
Save when your own imperious branches swinging,
   Have made a solemn music of the wind!
Where, like a man beloved of God,
Through glooms, which never woodman trod,
    How oft, pursuing fancies holy,   10
My moonlight way o'er flowering weeds I wound,
    Inspired, beyond the guess of folly,

V

The Sensual and the Dark rebel in vain,
  Slaves by their own compulsion! In mad game
They burst their manacles and wear the name
  Of Freedom, graven on a heavier chain!
O Liberty! with profitless endeavour
Have I pursued thee, many a weary hour;   90
  But thou nor swell'st the victor's strain, nor ever
Didst breathe thy soul in forms of human power.

  Alike from all, howe'er they praise thee,
    (Nor prayer, nor boastful name delays thee)
     Alike from Priestcraft's harpy minions,
  And factious Blasphemy's obscener slaves,
     Thou speedest on thy subtle pinions,
The guide of homeless winds, and playmate of the waves!
And there I felt thee!—on that sea-cliff's verge,
  Whose pines, scarce travelled by the breeze above,   100
Had made one murmur with the distant surge!
Yes, while I stood and gazed, my temples bare,
And shot my being through earth, sea, and air,
   Possessing all things with intensest love,
     O Liberty! my spirit felt thee there.

Fears in Solitude

WRITTEN IN APRIL 1798, DURING
THE ALARM OF AN INVASION

A green and silent spot, amid the hills,*
A small and silent dell! O'er stiller place
No singing sky-lark ever poised himself.
The hills are heathy, save that swelling slope,
Which hath a gay and gorgeous covering on,
All golden with the never-bloomless furze,
Which now blooms most profusely: but the dell,
Bathed by the mist, is fresh and delicate
As vernal corn-field, or the unripe flax,

When, through its half-transparent stalks, at eve,   10
The level sunshine glimmers with green light.
Oh! 'tis a quiet spirit-healing nook!
Which all, methinks, would love; but chiefly he,
The humble man, who, in his youthful years,
Knew just so much of folly, as had made
His early manhood more securely wise!
Here he might lie on fern or withered heath,
While from the singing lark (that sings unseen
The minstrelsy that solitude loves best),
And from the sun, and from the breezy air,   20
Sweet influences trembled o'er his frame;
And he, with many feelings, many thoughts,
Made up a meditative joy, and found
Religious meanings in the forms of Nature!
And so, his senses gradually wrapt
In a half sleep, he dreams of better worlds,
And dreaming hears thee still, O singing lark,
That singest like an angel in the clouds!

  My God! it is a melancholy thing
For such a man, who would full fain preserve   30
His soul in calmness, yet perforce must feel
For all his human brethren—O my God!
It weighs upon the heart, that he must think
What uproar and what strife may now be stirring
This way or that way o'er these silent hills—
Invasion, and the thunder and the shout,
And all the crash of onset; fear and rage,
And undetermined conflict—even now,
Even now, perchance, and in his native isle:
Carnage and groans beneath this blessed sun!   40
We have offended, Oh! my countrymen!
We have offended very grievously,
And been most tyrannous. From east to west
A groan of accusation pierces Heaven!
The wretched plead against us; multitudes
Countless and vehement, the sons of God,

As though he had no wife to pine for him,
No God to judge him! Therefore, evil days
Are coming on us, O my countrymen!
And what if all-avenging Providence,
Strong and retributive, should make us know
The meaning of our words, force us to feel
The desolation and the agony
Of our fierce doings?

    Spare us yet awhile,
Father and God! O spare us yet awhile!   130
Oh! let not English women drag their flight
Fainting beneath the burthen of their babes,
Of the sweet infants, that but yesterday
Laughed at the breast! Sons, brothers, husbands, all
Who ever gazed with fondness on the forms
Which grew up with you round the same fire-side,
And all who ever heard the sabbath-bells
Without the infidel's scorn, make yourselves pure!   70
Stand forth! be men! repel an impious foe,
Impious and false, a light yet cruel race,   14(
Who laugh away all virtue, mingling mirth
With deeds of murder; and still promising
Freedom, themselves too sensual to be free,
Poison life's amities, and cheat the heart
Of faith and quiet hope, and all that soothes,
And all that lifts the spirit! Stand we forth;
Render them back upon the insulted ocean,
And let them toss as idly on its waves
As the vile sea-weed, which some mountain-blast
Swept from our shores! And oh! may we return   150
Not with a drunken triumph, but with fear,
Repenting of the wrongs with which we stung
So fierce a foe to frenzy!

    I have told,
O Britons! O my brethren! I have told
Most bitter truth, but without bitterness.
Nor deem my zeal or factious or mistimed;

For never can true courage dwell with them,
Who, playing tricks with conscience, dare not look
At their own vices. We have been too long
Dupes of a deep delusion! Some, belike,   160
Groaning with restless enmity, expect
All change from change of constituted power;
As if a Government had been a robe,
On which our vice and wretchedness were tagged
Like fancy-points and fringes, with the robe
Pulled off at pleasure. Fondly these attach
A radical causation to a few
Poor drudges of chastising Providence,
Who borrow all their hues and qualities
From our own folly and rank wickedness,   170
Which gave them birth and nursed them. Others, mean-
    while,
Dote with a mad idolatry; and all
Who will not fall before their images,
And yield them worship, they are enemies
Even of their country!

                    Such have I been deemed.—
But, O dear Britain! O my Mother Isle!
Needs must thou prove a name most dear and holy
To me, a son, a brother, and a friend,
A husband, and a father! who revere
All bonds of natural love, and find them all   180
Within the limits of thy rocky shores.
O native Britain! O my Mother Isle!
How shouldst thou prove aught else but dear and holy
To me, who from thy lakes and mountain-hills,
Thy clouds, thy quiet dales, thy rocks and seas,
Have drunk in all my intellectual life,
All sweet sensations, all ennobling thoughts,
All adoration of the God in nature,
All lovely and all honourable things,
Whatever makes this mortal spirit feel   190
The joy and greatness of its future being?
There lives nor form nor feeling in my soul

Unborrowed from my country! O divine
And beauteous island! thou hast been my sole
And most magnificent temple, in the which
I walk with awe, and sing my stately songs,
Loving the God that made me!—

                                    May my fears,
My filial fears, be vain! and may the vaunts
And menace of the vengeful enemy
Pass like the gust, that roared and died away   200
In the distant tree: which heard, and only heard
In this low dell, bowed not the delicate grass.

    But now the gentle dew-fall sends abroad
The fruit-like perfume of the golden furze:
The light has left the summit of the hill,
Though still a sunny gleam lies beautiful,
Aslant the ivied beacon. Now farewell,
Farewell, awhile, O soft and silent spot!
On the green sheep-track, up the heathy hill,
Homeward I wind my way; and lo! recalled   210
From bodings that have well-nigh wearied me,
I find myself upon the brow, and pause
Startled! And after lonely sojourning
In such a quiet and surrounded nook,
This burst of prospect, here the shadowy main,
Dim-tinted, there the mighty majesty
Of that huge amphitheatre of rich
And elmy fields, seems like society—
Conversing with the mind, and giving it
A livelier impulse and a dance of thought!   220
And now, belovéd Stowey! I behold
Thy church-tower, and, methinks, the four huge elms
Clustering, which mark the mansion of my friend;
And close behind them, hidden from my view,
Is my own lowly cottage, where my babe
And my babe's mother dwell in peace! With light
And quickened footsteps thitherward I tend,
Remembering thee, O green and silent dell!

                              [*Fears in Solitude*]   93

And grateful, that by nature's quietness
And solitary musings, all my heart   230
Is softened, and made worthy to indulge
Love, and the thoughts that yearn for human kind.

The Nightingale

A CONVERSATION POEM, APRIL, 1798

No cloud, no relique of the sunken day
Distinguishes the West, no long thin slip
Of sullen light, no obscure trembling hues.
Come, we will rest on this old mossy bridge!
You see the glimmer of the stream beneath,
But hear no murmuring: it flows silently,
O'er its soft bed of verdure. All is still,
A balmy night! and though the stars be dim,
Yet let us think upon the vernal showers
That gladden the green earth, and we shall find   10
A pleasure in the dimness of the stars.
And hark! the Nightingale begins its song,
"Most musical, most melancholy" bird! *
A melancholy bird? Oh! idle thought!
In Nature there is nothing melancholy.
But some night-wandering man whose heart was pierced
With the remembrance of a grievous wrong,
Or slow distemper, or neglected love,
(And so, poor wretch! filled all things with himself,
And made all gentle sounds tell back the tale   20
Of his own sorrow) he, and such as he,
First named these notes a melancholy strain.
And many a poet echoes the conceit;
Poet who hath been building up the rhyme
When he had better far have stretched his limbs
Beside a brook in mossy forest-dell,
By sun or moon-light, to the influxes
Of shapes and sounds and shifting elements
Surrendering his whole spirit, of his song

And of his fame forgetful! so his fame   30
Should share in Nature's immortality,
A venerable thing! and so his song
Should make all Nature lovelier, and itself
Be loved like Nature! But 'twill not be so;
And youths and maidens most poetical,
Who lose the deepening twilights of the spring
In ball-rooms and hot theatres, they still
Full of meek sympathy must heave their sighs
O'er Philomela's pity-pleading strains.*

My friend, and thou, our Sister! we have learnt   40
A different lore: we may not thus profane
Nature's sweet voices, always full of love
And joyance! 'Tis the merry Nightingale
That crowds, and hurries, and precipitates
With fast thick warble his delicious notes,
As he were fearful that an April night,
Would be too short for him to utter forth
His love-chant, and disburthen his full soul
Of all its music!

           And I know a grove
Of large extent, hard by a castle huge,
Which the great lord inhabits not; and so   50
This grove is wild with tangling underwood,
And the trim walks are broken up, and grass,
Thin grass and king-cups grow within the paths.
But never elsewhere in one place I knew
So many nightingales; and far and near,
In wood and thicket, over the wide grove,
They answer and provoke each other's song,
With skirmish and capricious passagings,
And murmurs musical and swift jug jug,   60
And one low piping sound more sweet than all—
Stirring the air with such a harmony,
That should you close your eyes, you might almost
Forget it was not day! On moonlight bushes,
Whose dewy leaflets are but half-disclosed,

You may perchance behold them on the twigs,
Their bright, bright eyes, their eyes both bright and full,
Glistening, while many a glow-worm in the shade
Lights up her love-torch.

               A most gentle Maid,
Who dwelleth in her hospitable home   70
Hard by the castle, and at latest eve
(Even like a Lady vowed and dedicate
To something more than Nature in the grove)
Glides through the pathways; she knows all their notes,
That gentle Maid! and oft, a moment's space,
What time the moon was lost behind a cloud,
Hath heard a pause of silence; till the moon
Emerging, hath awakened earth and sky
With one sensation, and those wakeful birds
Have all burst forth in choral minstrelsy,   80
As if some sudden gale had swept at once
A hundred airy harps! And she hath watched
Many a nightingale perch giddily
On blossomy twig still swinging from the breeze,
And to that motion tune his wanton song
Like tipsy Joy that reels with tossing head.

Farewell, O Warbler! till to-morrow eve,
And you, my friends! farewell, a short farewell!
We have been loitering long and pleasantly,
And now for our dear homes.—That strain again!   90
Full fain it would delay me! My dear babe,
Who, capable of no articulate sound,
Mars all things with his imitative lisp,
How he would place his hand beside his ear,
His little hand, the small forefinger up,
And bid us listen! And I deem it wise
To make him Nature's play-mate. He knows well
The evening-star; and once, when he awoke
In most distressful mood (some inward pain
Had made up that strange thing, an infant's dream—)
I hurried with him to our orchard-plot,   101

Contents

5

And he beheld the moon, and, hushed at once,
Suspends his sobs, and laughs most silently,
While his fair eyes, that swam with undropped tears,
Did glitter in the yellow moon-beam! Well!—
It is a father's tale: But if that Heaven
Should give me life, his childhood shall grow up
Familiar with these songs, that with the night
He may associate joy.—Once more, farewell,
Sweet Nightingale! once more, my friends! farewell.   110

The Wanderings of Cain

PREFATORY NOTE

A prose composition, one not in metre at least, seems
primâ facie to require explanation or apology. It was written in the year 1798, near Nether Stowey, in Somersetshire, at which place (sanctum et amabile nomen! rich
by so many associations and recollections) the author had
taken up his residence in order to enjoy the society and
close neighbourhood of a dear and honoured friend, T.
Poole, Esq. The work was to have been written in concert
with another [Wordsworth], whose name is too venerable
within the precincts of genius to be unnecessarily brought
into connection with such a trifle, and who was then re-
siding at a small distance from Nether Stowey. The title
and subject were suggested by myself, who likewise drew
out the scheme and the contents for each of the three
books or cantos, of which the work was to consist, and
which, the reader is to be informed, was to have been finished in one night! My partner undertook the first canto: I
the second: and which ever had done first, was to set
about the third. Almost thirty years have passed by; yet at
this moment I cannot without something more than a
smile moot the question which of the two things was the
more impracticable, for a mind so eminently original to
compose another man's thoughts and fancies, or for a
taste so austerely pure and simple to imitate the Death of

Abel? [1] Methinks I see his grand and noble countenance as at the moment when having despatched my own portion of the task at full finger-speed, I hastened to him with my manuscript—that look of humorous despondency fixed on his almost blank sheet of paper, and then its silent mock-piteous admission of failure struggling with the sense of the exceeding ridiculousness of the whole scheme—which broke up in a laugh: and the Ancient Mariner was written instead.

Years afterward, however, the draft of the plan and proposed incidents, and the portion executed, obtained favour in the eyes of more than one person, whose judgment on a poetic work could not but have weighed with me, even though no parental partiality had been thrown into the same scale, as a make-weight: and I determined on commencing anew, and composing the whole in stanzas, and made some progress in realising this intention, when adverse gales drove my bark off the "Fortunate Isles" of the Muses: and then other and more momentous interests prompted a different voyage, to firmer anchorage and a securer port. I have in vain tried to recover the lines from the palimpsest tablet of my memory: and I can only offer the introductory stanza, which had been committed to writing for the purpose of procuring a friend's judgment on the metre, as a specimen:—

> Encinctured with a twine of leaves,
> That leafy twine his only dress!
> A lovely Boy was plucking fruits,
> By moonlight, in a wilderness.
> The moon was bright, the air was free,
> And fruits and flowers together grew
> On many a shrub and many a tree:
> And all put on a gentle hue,
> Hanging in the shadowy air
> Like a picture rich and rare.
> It was a climate where, they say,

1. *The Death of Abel* is a work by the eighteenth-century Swiss poet, Solomon Gessner.

The night is more belov'd than day.
But who that beauteous Boy beguil'd,
That beauteous Boy to linger here?
Alone, by night, a little child,
In place so silent and so wild—
Has he no friend, no loving mother near?

*I have here given the birth, parentage, and premature
decease of the "Wanderings of Cain, a poem",—intreating,
however, my Readers, not to think so meanly of my judgment as to suppose that I either regard or offer it as any
excuse for the publication of the following fragment (and
I may add, of one or two others in its neighbourhood) in
its primitive crudity. But I should find still greater diffi-
culty in forgiving myself were I to record pro taedio pub-
lico a set of petty mishaps and annoyances which I myself
wish to forget. I must be content therefore with assuring
the friendly Reader, that the less he attributes its appearance to the Author's will, choice, or judgment, the nearer
to the truth he will be.*

S. T. COLERIDGE (1828).

CANTO II

"A little further, O my father, yet a little further, and
we shall come into the open moonlight." Their road was
through a forest of fir-trees; at its entrance the trees stood
at distances from each other, and the path was broad, and
the moonlight and the moonlight shadows reposed upon it,
and appeared quietly to inhabit that solitude. But soon the
path winded and became narrow; the sun at high noon
sometimes speckled, but never illumined it, and now it
was dark as a cavern.

"It is dark, O my father!" said Enos, "but the path under
our feet is smooth and soft, and we shall soon come out
into the open moonlight."

"Lead on, my child!" said Cain; "guide me, little child!"
And the innocent little child clasped a finger of the hand
which had murdered the righteous Abel, and he guided his
father. "The fir branches drip upon thee, my son." "Yea,

pleasantly, father, for I ran fast and eagerly to bring thee the pitcher and the cake, and my body is not yet cool. How happy the squirrels are that feed on these fir-trees! they leap from bough to bough, and the old squirrels play round their young ones in the nest. I clomb a tree yesterday at noon, O my father, that I might play with them, but they leaped away from the branches, even to the slender twigs did they leap, and in a moment I beheld them on another tree. Why, O my father, would they not play with me? I would be good to them as thou art good to me: and I groaned to them even as thou groanest when thou givest me to eat, and when thou coverest me at evening, and as often as I stand at thy knee and thine eyes look at me?" Then Cain stopped, and stifling his groans he sank to the earth, and the child Enos stood in the darkness beside him.

And Cain lifted up his voice and cried bitterly, and said, "The Mighty One that persecuteth me is on this side and on that; he pursueth my soul like the wind, like the sand-blast he passeth through me; he is around me even as the air! O that I might be utterly no more! I desire to die—yea, the things that never had life, neither move they upon the earth—behold! they seem precious to mine eyes. O that a man might live without the breath of his nostrils. So I might abide in darkness, and blackness, and an empty space! Yea, I would lie down. I would not rise, neither would I stir my limbs till I became as the rock in the den of the lion, on which the young lion resteth his head whilst he sleepeth. For the torrent that roareth far off hath a voice: and the clouds in heaven look terribly on me; the Mighty One who is against me speaketh in the wind of the cedar grove; and in silence am I dried up." Then Enos spake to his father, "Arise, my father, arise, we are but a little way from the place where I found the cake and the pitcher." And Cain said, "How knowest thou!" and the child answered—"Behold the bare rocks are a few of thy strides distant from the forest; and while even now thou wert lifting up thy voice, I heard the echo." Then the child took hold of his father, as if he would raise him: and Cain being faint and feeble rose slowly on his knees and pressed himself against the trunk of a fir, and stood upright and followed the child.

The path was dark till within three strides' length of its termination, when it turned suddenly; the thick black trees formed a low arch, and the moonlight appeared for a moment like a dazzling portal. Enos ran before and stood in the open air; and when Cain, his father, emerged from the darkness, the child was affrighted. For the mighty limbs of Cain were wasted as by fire; his hair was as the matted curls on the bison's forehead, and so glared his fierce and sullen eye beneath: and the black abundant locks on either side, a rank and tangled mass, were stained and scorched, as though the grasp of a burning iron hand had striven to rend them; and his countenance told in a strange and terrible language of agonies that had been, and were, and were still to continue to be.

The scene around was desolate; as far as the eye could reach it was desolate: the bare rocks faced each other, and left a long and wide interval of thin white sand. You might wander on and look round and round, and peep into the crevices of the rocks and discover nothing that acknowledged the influence of the seasons. There was no spring, no summer, no autumn: and the winter's snow, that would have been lovely, fell not on these hot rocks and scorching sands. Never morning lark had poised himself over this desert; but the huge serpent often hissed there beneath the talons of the vulture, and the vulture screamed, his wings imprisoned within the coils of the serpent. The pointed and shattered summits of the ridges of the rocks made a rude mimicry of human concerns, and seemed to prophesy mutely of things that then were not; steeples, and battlements, and ships with naked masts. As far from the wood as a boy might sling a pebble of the brook, there was one rock by itself at a small distance from the main ridge. It had been precipitated there perhaps by the groan which the Earth uttered when our first father fell. Before you approached, it appeared to lie flat on the ground, but its base slanted from its point, and between its point and the sands a tall man might stand upright. It was here that Enos had found the pitcher and cake, and to this place he led his father. But ere they had reached the rock they beheld a human shape: his back was towards them, and they were advancing and unperceived, when they heard him smite his breast and cry aloud, "Woe is me! woe is me! I must never die again, and yet I am perishing with thirst and hunger."

Pallid, as the reflection of the sheeted lightning on the heavy-sailing night-cloud, became the face of Cain; but the child Enos took hold of the shaggy skin, his father's robe, and raised his eyes to his father, and listening whispered, "Ere yet I could speak, I am sure, O my father, that I heard that voice. Have not I often said that I remembered a sweet voice? O my father! this is it": and Cain trembled exceedingly. The voice was sweet indeed, but it was thin and querulous, like that of a feeble slave in misery, who despairs altogether, yet can not refrain himself from weeping and lamentation. And, behold! Enos glided forward, and creeping softly round the base of the rock, stood before the stranger, and looked up into his face. And the Shape shrieked, and turned round, and Cain beheld him, that his limbs and his face were those of his brother Abel whom he had killed! [2] And Cain stood like one who struggles in his sleep because of the exceeding terribleness of a dream.

Thus as he stood in silence and darkness of soul, the Shape fell at his feet, and embraced his knees, and cried out with a bitter outcry, "Thou eldest born of Adam, whom Eve, my mother, brought forth, cease to torment me! I was feeding my flocks in green pastures by the side of quiet rivers, and thou killedst me; and now I am in misery." Then Cain closed his eyes, and hid them with his hands; and again he opened his eyes, and looked around him, and said to Enos, "What beholdest thou? Didst thou

2. Some of Coleridge's MS notes suggest that the Shape resembling Abel was to be an evil spirit attempting to deceive Cain into sacrificing Enos.

hear a voice, my son?" "Yes, my father, I beheld a man in unclean garments, and he uttered a sweet voice, full of lamentation." Then Cain raised up the Shape that was like Abel, and said:—"The Creator of our father, who had respect unto thee, and unto thy offering, wherefore hath he forsaken thee?" Then the Shape shrieked a second time, and rent his garment, and his naked skin was like the white sands beneath their feet; and he shrieked yet a third time, and threw himself on his face upon the sand that was black with the shadow of the rock, and Cain and Enos sate beside him; the child by his right hand, and Cain by his left. They were all three under the rock, and within the shadow. The Shape that was like Abel raised himself up, and spake to the child, "I know where the cold waters are, but I may not drink, wherefore didst thou then take away my pitcher?" But Cain said, "Didst thou not find favour in the sight of the Lord thy God?" The Shape answered, "The Lord is God of the living only, the dead have another God." Then the child Enos lifted up his eyes and prayed; but Cain rejoiced secretly in his heart. "Wretched shall they be all the days of their mortal life," exclaimed the Shape, "who sacrifice worthy and acceptable sacrifices to the God of the dead; but after death their toil ceaseth. Woe is me, for I was well beloved by the God of the living, and cruel wert thou, O my brother, who didst snatch me away from his power and his dominion." Having uttered these words, he rose suddenly, and fled over the sands: and Cain said in his heart, "The curse of the Lord is on me; but who is the God of the dead?" and he ran after the Shape, and the Shape fled shrieking over the sands, and the sands rose like white mists behind the steps of Cain, but the feet of him that was like Abel disturbed not the sands. He greatly outrun Cain, and turning short, he wheeled round, and came again to the rock where they had been sitting, and where Enos still stood; and the child caught hold of his garment as he passed by, and he fell upon the ground. And Cain stopped, and beholding him not, said, "he has passed into the dark woods," and he walked slowly back to the rocks; and when he reached it the child told him that he had caught hold of his garment as he passed by, and that the man had fallen upon the ground: and Cain once more sate beside him, and said, "Abel, my brother, I would lament for thee, but that the spirit within me is withered, and burnt up with extreme agony. Now, I pray thee, by thy flocks, and by thy pastures, and by the quiet rivers which thou lovedst, that thou tell me all that thou knowest. Who is the God of the dead? where doth he make his dwelling? what sacrifices are acceptable unto him? for I have offered, but have not been received; I have prayed, and have not been heard; and how can I be afflicted more than I already am?" The Shape arose and answered, "O that thou hadst had pity on me as I will have pity on thee. Follow me, Son of Adam! and bring thy child with thee!"

And they three passed over the white sands between the rocks, silent as the shadows.

The Ballad of the Dark Ladié

A FRAGMENT

Beneath yon birch with silver bark,*
And boughs so pendulous and fair,
The brook falls scatter'd down the rock:
    And all is mossy there!

And there upon the moss she sits,
The Dark Ladié in silent pain;
The heavy tear is in her eye,
    And drops and swells again.

Three times she sends her little page
Up the castled mountain's breast,   10
If he might find the Knight that wears
    The Griffin for his crest.

The sun was sloping down the sky,

And she had linger'd there all day,
Counting moments, dreaming fears—
 Oh wherefore can he stay?

She hears a rustling o'er the brook,
She sees far off a swinging bough!
" 'Tis He! 'Tis my betrothéd Knight!
 Lord Falkland, it is Thou!"   20

She springs, she clasps him round the neck,
She sobs a thousand hopes and fears,
Her kisses glowing on his cheeks
 She quenches with her tears.

 *   *   *   *

"My friends with rude ungentle words
They scoff and bid me fly to thee!
O give me shelter in thy breast!
 O shield and shelter me!

"My Henry, I have given thee much,
I gave what I can ne'er recall,   30
I gave my heart, I gave my peace,
 O Heaven! I gave thee all."

The Knight made answer to the Maid,
While to his heart he held her hand,
"Nine castles hath my noble sire,
 None statelier in the land.

"The Fairest one shall be my love's,
The fairest castle of the nine!
Wait only till the stars peep out,
 The fairest shall be thine: 40

"Wait only till the hand of eve
Hath wholly closed yon western bars,
And through the dark we two will steal
 Beneath the twinkling stars!"—

"The dark? the dark? No! not the dark?
The twinkling stars? How, Henry? How?"
O God! 'twas in the eye of noon
    He pledged his sacred vow!

And in the eye of noon my love
Shall lead me from my mother's door,   50
Sweet boys and girls all clothed in white
    Strewing flowers before:

But first the nodding minstrels go
With music meet for lordly bowers,
The children next in snow-white vests,
    Strewing buds and flowers!

And then my love and I shall pace,
My jet black hair in pearly braids,
Between our comely bachelors   60
    And blushing bridal maids.

    *   *   *   *

Kubla Khan

OR, A VISION IN A DREAM. A FRAGMENT.

*The following fragment is here published at the request of
a poet of great and deserved celebrity [Lord Byron], and,
as far as the Author's own opinions are concerned, rather
as a psychological curiosity, than on the ground of any
supposed poetic merits.*

   *In the summer of the year 1797, the Author, then in ill
health, had retired to a lonely farm-house between Porlock
and Linton, on the Exmoor confines of Somerset and Devonshire. In consequence of a slight indisposition, an ano-
dyne had been prescribed, from the effects of which he
fell asleep in his chair at the moment that he was reading
the following sentence, or words of the same substance,
in "Purchas's Pilgrimage": "Here the Khan Kubla com-*

manded a palace to be built, and a stately garden there-unto. And thus ten miles of fertile ground were inclosed with a wall." The Author continued for about three hours in a profound sleep, at least of the external senses, during which time he has the most vivid confidence, that he could not have composed less than from two to three hundred lines; if that indeed can be called composition in which all the images rose up before him as things, with a parallel production of the correspondent expressions, without any sensation or consciousness of effort. On awaking he appeared to himself to have a distinct recollection of the whole, and taking his pen, ink, and paper, instantly and eagerly wrote down the lines that are here preserved. At this moment he was unfortunately called out by a person on business from Porlock, and detained by him above an hour, and on his return to his room, found, to his no small surprise and mortification, that though he still retained some vague and dim recollection of the general purport of the vision, yet, with the exception of some eight or ten scattered lines and images, all the rest had passed away like the images on the surface of a stream into which a stone has been cast, but, alas! without the after restoration of the latter!

> Then all the charm
> Is broken—all that phantom-world so fair
> Vanishes, and a thousand circlets spread,
> And each mis-shape['s] the other. Stay awhile,
> Poor youth! who scarcely dar'st lift up thine eyes—
> The stream will soon renew its smoothness, soon
> The visions will return! And lo, he stays,
> And soon the fragments dim of lovely forms
> Come trembling back, unite, and now once more
> The pool becomes a mirror.[1]

Yet from the still surviving recollections in his mind, the Author has frequently purposed to finish for himself what had been originally, as it were, given to him.

1. Lines from Coleridge's poem, "The Picture."

Σαμερου αδιογ ασω: [2] but the to-morrow is yet to come.

KUBLA KHAN

In Xanadu did Kubla Khan
A stately pleasure-dome decree:
Where Alph, the sacred river, ran
Through caverns measureless to man
   Down to a sunless sea.
So twice five miles of fertile ground
With walls and towers were girdled round:
And there were gardens bright with sinuous rills,
Where blossomed many an incense-bearing tree;
And here were forests ancient as the hills,   10
Enfolding sunny spots of greenery.

But oh! that deep romantic chasm which slanted
Down the green hill athwart a cedarn cover!
A savage place! as holy and enchanted
As e'er beneath a waning moon was haunted
By woman wailing for her demon-lover!
And from this chasm, with ceaseless turmoil seething,
As if this earth in fast thick pants were breathing,
A mighty fountain momently was forced:
Amid whose swift half-intermitted burst   20
Huge fragments vaulted like rebounding hail,
Or chaffy grain beneath the thresher's flail:
And 'mid these dancing rocks at once and ever
It flung up momently the sacred river.
Five miles meandering with a mazy motion
Through wood and dale the sacred river ran,
Then reached the caverns measureless to man,
And sank in tumult to a lifeless ocean:
And 'mid this tumult Kubla heard from far
Ancestral voices prophesying war!   30

   2. The quotation, from Theocritus, *Idylls*, I, 132, means:
"to sing a sweeter song tomorrow."

The shadow of the dome of pleasure
Floated midway on the waves;
Where was heard the mingled measure
From the fountain and the caves.
It was a miracle of rare device,
A sunny pleasure-dome with caves of ice!

A damsel with a dulcimer
In a vision once I saw:
It was an Abyssinian maid,
And on her dulcimer she played,   40
Singing of Mount Abora.
Could I revive within me
Her symphony and song,
To such a deep delight 'twould win me,
That with music loud and long,
I would build that dome in air,
That sunny dome! those caves of ice!
And all who heard should see them there,
And all should cry, Beware! Beware!
His flashing eyes, his floating hair!   50
Weave a circle round him thrice,
And close your eyes with holy dread,
For he on honey-dew hath fed,
And drunk the milk of Paradise.

Hexameters

William, my teacher, my friend! dear William and
    dear Dorothea! *
Smooth out the folds of my letter, and place it on desk or
    on table;
Place it on table or desk; and your right hands loosely
    half-closing,
Gently sustain them in air, and extending the digit didac-
    tic,
Rest it a moment on each of the forks of the five-forkéd
    left hand,

Twice on the breadth of the thumb, and once on the tip
of each finger;
Read with a nod of the head in a humouring recitativo;
And, as I live, you will see my hexameters hopping before
you.
This is a galloping measure; a hop, and a trot, and a
gallop!

All my hexameters fly, like stags pursued by the stag-
hounds,   10
Breathless and panting, and ready to drop, yet flying still
onwards,
I would full fain pull in my hard-mouthed runaway
hunter;
But our English Spondeans are clumsy yet impotent curb-
reins;
And so to make him go slowly, no way left have I but to
lame him.

William, my head and my heart! dear Poet that feelest
and thinkest!
Dorothy, eager of soul, my most affectionate sister!
Many a mile, O! many a wearisome mile are ye distant,
Long, long comfortless roads, with no one eye that doth
know us.
O! it is all too far to send you mockeries idle:
Yea, and I feel it not right! But O! my friends, my be-
lovéd!   20
Feverish and wakeful I lie,—I am weary of feeling and
thinking.
Every thought is worn *down*, I am weary yet cannot be
vacant.
Five long hours have I tossed, rheumatic heats, dry and
flushing,
Gnawing behind in my head, and wandering and throb-
bing about me,
Busy and tiresome, my friends, as the beat of the boding
night-spider.

I forget the beginning of the line:

. . . my eyes are a burthen,
Now unwillingly closed, now open and aching with dark-
　　ness.
O! what a life is the eye! what a strange and inscrutable
　　essence!
Him that is utterly blind, nor glimpses the fire that warms
　　him;　　　　　　　　　　　　　　　　　　　　　　29
Him that never beheld the swelling breast of his mother;
Him that smiled in his gladness as a babe that smiles in
　　its slumber;
Even for him it exists, it moves and stirs in its prison;
Lives with a separate life, and "Is it a Spirit?" he mur-
　　murs:
"Sure it has thoughts of its own, and to see is only a lan-
　　guage."

There was a great deal more, which I have forgotten.
. . . The last line which I wrote, I remember, and write it
for the truth of the sentiment, scarcely less true in com-
pany than in pain and solitude:—

William, my head and my heart! dear William and
　　dear Dorothea!
You have all in each other; but I am lonely, and want you!

Lines

WRITTEN IN THE ALBUM AT ELBINGERODE,
IN THE HARTZ FOREST

I stood on Brocken's sovran height, and saw
Woods crowding upon woods, hills over hills,
A surging scene, and only limited
By the blue distance. Heavily my way
Downward I dragged through fir groves evermore,

Where bright green moss heaves in sepulchral forms
Speckled with sunshine; and, but seldom heard,
The sweet bird's song became a hollow sound;
And the breeze, murmuring indivisibly,
Preserved its solemn murmur most distinct   10
From many a note of many a waterfall,
And the brook's chatter; 'mid whose islet-stones
The dingy kidling with its tinkling bell
Leaped frolicsome, or old romantic goat
Sat, his white beard slow waving. I moved on
In low and languid mood: for I had found
That outward forms, the loftiest, still receive
Their finer influence from the Life within;—
Fair cyphers else: fair, but of import vague
Or unconcerning, where the heart not finds   20
History or prophecy of friend, or child,
Or gentle maid, our first and early love,
Or father, or the venerable name
Of our adoréd country! O thou Queen,
Thou delegated Deity of Earth,
O dear, dear England! how my longing eye
Turned westward, shaping in the steady clouds
Thy sands and high white cliffs!

                                      My native Land!
Filled with the thought of thee this heart was proud,   30
Yea, mine eye swam with tears: that all the view
From sovran Brocken, woods and woody hills,
Floated away, like a departing dream,
Feeble and dim! Stranger, these impulses
Blame thou not lightly; nor will I profane,
With hasty judgment or injurious doubt,
That man's sublimer spirit, who can feel
That God is everywhere! the God who framed
Mankind to be one mighty family,
Himself our Father, and the World our Home.   40

Love

All thoughts, all passions, all delights,*
Whatever stirs this mortal frame,
All are but ministers of Love,
  And feed his sacred flame.

Oft in my waking dreams do I
Live o'er again that happy hour,
When midway on the mount I lay,
  Beside the ruined tower.

The moonshine, stealing o'er the scene
Had blended with the lights of eve;   10
And she was there, my hope, my joy,
  My own dear Genevieve!

She leant against the arméd man
The statue of the arméd knight;
She stood and listened to my lay,
  Amid the lingering light.

Few sorrows hath she of her own,
My hope! my joy! my Genevieve!
She loves me best, whene'er I sing
  The songs that make her grieve.   20

I played a soft and doleful air,
I sang an old and moving story—
An old rude song, that suited well
  That ruin wild and hoary.

She listened with a flitting blush,
With downcast eyes and modest grace;
For well she knew, I could not choose
  But gaze upon her face.

I told her of the Knight that wore
Upon his shield a burning brand;   30

And that for ten long years he wooed
    The Lady of the Land.

I told her how he pined: and ah!
The deep, the low, the pleading tone
With which I sang another's love,
    Interpreted my own.

She listened with a flitting blush,
With downcast eyes, and modest grace;
And she forgave me, that I gazed
    Too fondly on her face!   40

But when I told the cruel scorn
That crazed that bold and lovely Knight,
And that he crossed the mountain-woods,
    Nor rested day nor night;

That sometimes from the savage den,
And sometimes from the darksome shade,
And sometimes starting up at once
    In green and sunny glade,—

There came and looked him in the face
An angel beautiful and bright;   50
And that he knew it was a Fiend,
    This miserable Knight!

And that unknowing what he did,
He leaped amid a murderous band,
And saved from outrage worse than death
    The Lady of the Land!

And how she wept, and clasped his knees;
And how she tended him in vain—
And ever strove to expiate
    The scorn that crazed his brain;—   60

And that she nursed him in a cave;

And how his madness went away,
When on the yellow forest-leaves
    A dying man he lay;—

His dying words—but when I reached
That tenderest strain of all the ditty,
My faultering voice and pausing harp
    Disturbed her soul with pity!

All impulses of soul and sense
Had thrilled my guileless Genevieve;   70
The music and the doleful tale,
    The rich and balmy eve;

And hopes, and fears that kindle hope,
An undistinguishable throng,
And gentle wishes long subdued,
    Subdued and cherished long!

She wept with pity and delight,
She blushed with love, and virgin-shame;
And like the murmur of a dream,
    I heard her breathe my name.   80

Her bosom heaved—she stepped aside,
As conscious of my look she stepped—
Then suddenly, with timorous eye
    She fled to me and wept.

She half enclosed me with her arms,
She pressed me with a meek embrace;
And bending back her head, looked up,
    And gazed upon my face.

'Twas partly love, and partly fear,
And partly 'twas a bashful art,   90
That I might rather feel, than see,
    The swelling of her heart.

I calmed her fears, and she was calm,
And told her love with virgin pride;
And so I won my Genevieve,
    My bright and beauteous Bride.

Apologia Pro Vita Sua

The Poet in his lone yet genial hour
Gives to his eyes a magnifying power:
Or rather he emancipates his eyes
From the black shapeless accidents of size—
In unctuous cones of kindling coal,
Or smoke upwreathing from the pipe's trim bole,
    His gifted ken can see
    Phantoms of sublimity.

Dejection: An Ode

[WRITTEN APRIL 4, 1802]

Late, late yestreen I saw the new Moon,
With the old Moon in her arms;
And I fear, I fear, my Master dear!
We shall have a deadly storm.
        BALLAD OF SIR PATRICK SPENCE

I

Well! If the Bard was weather-wise, who made *
    The grand old ballad of Sir Patrick Spence,
    This night, so tranquil now, will not go hence
Unroused by winds, that ply a busier trade
Than those which mould yon cloud in lazy flakes,
Or the dull sobbing draft, that moans and rakes
Upon the strings of this Aeolian lute,
    Which better far were mute.
    For lo! the New-moon winter-bright!
    And overspread with phantom light,
    (With swimming phantom light o'erspread

10

But rimmed and circled by a silver thread)
I see the old Moon in her lap, foretelling
   The coming-on of rain and squally blast.
And oh! that even now the gust were swelling,
   And the slant night-shower driving loud and fast!
Those sounds which oft have raised me, whilst they awed,
     And sent my soul abroad,
Might now perhaps their wonted impulse give,   19
Might startle this dull pain, and make it move and live!

     II

A grief without a pang, void, dark, and drear,
   A stifled, drowsy, unimpassioned grief,
   Which finds no natural outlet, no relief,
     In word, or sigh, or tear—
O Lady! in this wan and heartless mood,
To other thoughts by yonder throstle woo'd,
   All this long eve, so balmy and serene,
Have I been gazing on the western sky,
   And its peculiar tint of yellow green:
And still I gaze—and with how blank an eye!   30
And those thin clouds above, in flakes and bars,
That give away their motion to the stars;
Those stars, that glide behind them or between,
Now sparkling, now bedimmed, but always seen:
Yon crescent Moon, as fixed as if it grew
In its own cloudless, starless lake of blue;
I see them all so excellently fair,
I see, not feel, how beautiful they are!

     III

   My genial spirits fail;
   And what can these avail   40
To lift the smothering weight from off my breast?
   It were a vain endeavour,
   Though I should gaze for ever
On that green light that lingers in the west:
I may not hope from outward forms to win
The passion and the life, whose fountains are within.

             [Dejection: An Ode] 117

IV

O Lady! we receive but what we give,
And in our life alone does Nature live:
Ours is her wedding garment, ours her shroud!
   And would we aught behold, of higher worth,   50
Than that inanimate cold world allowed
To the poor loveless ever-anxious crowd,
   Ah! from the soul itself must issue forth
A light, a glory, a fair luminous cloud
      Enveloping the Earth—
And from the soul itself must there be sent
   A sweet and potent voice, of its own birth,
Of all sweet sounds the life and element!

V

O pure of heart! thou need'st not ask of me
What this strong music in the soul may be!   60
What, and wherein doth exist,
This light, this glory, this fair luminous mist,
This beautiful and beauty-making power.
   Joy, virtuous Lady! Joy that ne'er was given,
Save to the pure, and in their purest hour,
Life, and Life's effluence, cloud at once and shower,
Joy, Lady! is the spirit and the power,
Which wedding Nature to us gives in dower
   A new Earth and new Heaven,
Undreamt of by the sensual and the proud—   70
Joy is the sweet voice, Joy the luminous cloud—
      We in ourselves rejoice!
And thence flows all that charms or ear or sight,
   All melodies the echoes of that voice,
All colours a suffusion from that light.

VI

There was a time when, though my path was rough,
   This joy within me dallied with distress,
And all misfortunes were but as the stuff
   Whence Fancy made me dreams of happiness:

For hope grew round me, like the twining vine,   80
And fruits, and foliage, not my own, seemed mine.
But now afflictions bow me down to earth:
Nor care I that they rob me of my mirth;
  But oh! each visitation
Suspends what nature gave me at my birth,
 My shaping spirit of Imagination.
For not to think of what I needs must feel,
 But to be still and patient, all I can;
And haply by abstruse research to steal
 From my own nature all the natural man—   90
 This was my sole resource, my only plan:
Till that which suits a part infects the whole,
And now is almost grown the habit of my soul.

  VII

Hence, viper thoughts, that coil around my mind,
  Reality's dark dream!
I turn from you, and listen to the wind,
 Which long has raved unnoticed. What a scream
Of agony by torture lengthened out
That lute sent forth! Thou Wind, that rav'st without,
 Bare crag, or mountain-tairn, or blasted tree,   100
Or pine-grove whither woodman never clomb,
Or lonely house, long held the witches' home,
 Methinks were fitter instruments for thee,
Mad Lutanist! who in this month of showers,
Of dark-brown gardens, and of peeping flowers,
Mak'st Devils' yule, with worse than wintry song,
The blossoms, buds, and timorous leaves among.
 Thou Actor, perfect in all tragic sounds!
Thou mighty Poet, e'en to frenzy bold!
  What tell'st thou now about?   110
  'Tis of the rushing of an host in rout,
With groans, of trampled men, with smarting wounds—
At once they groan with pain, and shudder with the cold!
But hush! there is a pause of deepest silence!
 And all that noise, as of a rushing crowd,
With groans, and tremulous shudderings—all is over—

It tells another tale, with sounds less deep and loud!
    A tale of less affright,
    And tempered with delight,
As Otway's self had framed the tender lay,—*   120
    'Tis of a little child
    Upon a lonesome wild,
Not far from home, but she hath lost her way:
And now moans low in bitter grief and fear,
And now screams loud, and hopes to make her mother
    hear.

VIII

'Tis midnight, but small thoughts have I of sleep:
Full seldom may my friend such vigils keep!
Visit her, gentle Sleep! with wings of healing,
    And may this storm be but a mountain-birth,
May all the stars hang bright above her dwelling,   130
    Silent as though they watched the sleeping Earth!
    With light heart may she rise,
    Gay fancy, cheerful eyes,
    Joy lift her spirit, joy attune her voice;
To her may all things live, from pole to pole,
Their life the eddying of her living soul!
    O simple spirit, guided from above,
Dear Lady! friend devoutest of my choice,
Thus mayest thou ever, evermore rejoice.

The Picture

OR THE LOVER'S RESOLUTION

Through weeds and thorns, and matted underwood
I force my way; now climb, and now descend
O'er rocks, or bare or mossy, with wild foot
Crushing the purple whorts; while oft unseen,
Hurrying along the drifted forest-leaves,
The scared snake rustles. Onward still I toil,

I know not, ask not whither! A new joy,
Lovely as light, sudden as summer gust,
And gladsome as the first-born of the spring,
Beckons me on, or follows from behind,   10
Playmate, or guide! The master-passion quelled,
I feel that I am free. With dun-red bark
The fir-trees, and the unfrequent slender oak,
Forth from this tangle wild of bush and brake
Soar up, and form a melancholy vault
High o'er me, murmuring like a distant sea.

Here Wisdom might resort, and here Remorse;
Here too the love-lorn man, who, sick in soul,
And of this busy human heart aweary,
Worships the spirit of unconscious life   20
In tree or wild-flower.—Gentle lunatic!
If so he might not wholly cease to be,
He would far rather not be that he is;
But would be something that he knows not of,
In winds or waters, or among the rocks!

But hence, fond wretch! breathe not contagion here!
No myrtle-walks are these: these are no groves
Where Love dare loiter! If in sullen mood
He should stray hither, the low stumps shall gore
His dainty feet, the briar and the thorn   30
Make his plumes haggard. Like a wounded bird
Easily caught, ensnare him, O ye Nymphs,
Ye Oreads chaste, ye dusky Dryades;
And you, ye Earth-winds! you that make at morn
The dew-drops quiver on the spiders' webs!
You, O ye wingless Airs! that creep between
The rigid stems of heath and bitten furze,
Within whose scanty shade, at summer-noon,
The mother-sheep hath worn a hollow bed—
Ye, that now cool her fleece with dropless damp,   40
Now pant and murmur with her feeding lamb.
Chase, chase him, all ye Fays, and elfin Gnomes!
With prickles sharper than his darts bemock

His little Godship, making him perforce
Creep through a thorn-bush on yon hedgehog's back.

This is my hour of triumph! I can now
With my own fancies play the merry fool,
And laugh away worse folly, being free.
Here will I seat myself, beside this old,
Hollow, and weedy oak, which ivy-twine   50
Clothes as with net-work: here will I couch my limbs,
Close by this river, in this silent shade,
As safe and sacred from the step of man
As an invisible world—unheard, unseen,
And listening only to the pebbly brook
That murmurs with a dead, yet tinkling sound;
Or to the bees, that in the neighbouring trunk
Make honey-hoards. The breeze, that visits me,
Was never Love's accomplice, never raised
The tendril ringlets from the maiden's brow,   60
And the blue, delicate veins above her cheek;
Ne'er played the wanton—never half disclosed
The maiden's snowy bosom, scattering thence
Eye-poisons for some love-distempered youth,
Who ne'er henceforth may see an aspen-grove
Shiver in sunshine, but his feeble heart
Shall flow away like a dissolving thing.

Sweet breeze! thou only, if I guess aright,
Liftest the feathers of the robin's breast,
That swells its little breast, so full of song,   70
Singing above me, on the mountain-ash.
And thou too, desert stream! no pool of thine,
Though clear as lake in latest summer-eve,
Did e'er reflect the stately virgin's robe,
The face, the form divine, the downcast look
Contemplative! Behold! her open palm
Presses her cheek and brow! her elbow rests
On the bare branch of half-uprooted tree,
That leans towards its mirror! Who erewhile   79
Had from her countenance turned, or looked by stealth,

(For Fear is true-love's cruel nurse), he now
With steadfast gaze and unoffending eye,
Worships the watery idol, dreaming hopes
Delicious to the soul, but fleeting, vain,
E'en as that phantom-world on which he gazed,
But not unheeded gazed: for see, ah! see,
The sportive tyrant with her left hand plucks
The heads of tall flowers that behind her grow,
Lychnis, and willow-herb, and fox-glove bells:
And suddenly, as one that toys with time,   90
Scatters them on the pool! Then all the charm
Is broken—all that phantom world so fair
Vanishes, and a thousand circlets spread,
And each mis-shape the other. Stay awhile,
Poor youth, who scarcely dar'st lift up thine eyes!
The stream will soon renew its smoothness, soon
The visions will return! And lo! he stays:
And soon the fragments dim of lovely forms
Come trembling back, unite, and now once more
The pool becomes a mirror; and behold   100
Each wildflower on the marge inverted there,
And there the half-uprooted tree—but where,
O where the virgin's snowy arm, that leaned
On its bare branch? He turns, and she is gone!
Homeward she steals through many a woodland maze
Which he shall seek in vain. Ill-fated youth!
Go, day by day, and waste thy manly prime
In mad love-yearning by the vacant brook,
Till sickly thoughts bewitch thine eyes, and thou
Behold'st her shadow still abiding there,   110
The Naiad of the mirror!
                              Not to thee,
O wild and desert stream! belongs this tale:
Gloomy and dark art thou—the crowded firs
Spire from thy shores, and stretch across thy bed,
Making thee doleful as a cavern-well:
Save when the shy king-fishers build their nest
On thy steep banks, no loves hast thou, wild stream!
  This be my chosen haunt—emancipate

From Passion's dreams, a freeman, and alone,
I rise and trace its devious course. O lead,   120
Lead me to deeper shades and lonelier glooms.
Lo! stealing through the canopy of firs,
How fair the sunshine spots that mossy rock,
Isle of the river, whose disparted waves
Dart off asunder with an angry sound,
How soon to re-unite! And see! they meet,
Each in the other lost and found: and see
Placeless, as spirits, one soft water-sun
Throbbing within them, heart at once and eye!
With its soft neighbourhood of filmy clouds,   130
The stains and shadings of forgotten tears,
Dimness o'erswum with lustre! Such the hour
Of deep enjoyment, following love's brief feuds
And hark, the noise of a near waterfall!
I pass forth into light—I find myself
Beneath a weeping birch (most beautiful
Of forest trees, the Lady of the Woods),
Hard by the brink of a tall weedy rock
That overbrows the cataract. How bursts
The landscape on my sight! Two crescent hills   140
Fold in behind each other, and so make
A circular vale, and land-locked, as might seem,
With brook and bridge, and grey stone cottages,
Half hid by rocks and fruit-tress. At my feet,
The whortle-berries are bedewed with spray,
Dashed upwards by the furious waterfall.
How solemnly the pendent ivy-mass
Swings in its winnow: All the air is calm.
The smoke from cottage-chimneys, tinged with light,
Rises in columns; from this house alone,   150
Close by the water-fall, the column slants,
And feels its ceaseless breeze. But what is this?
That cottage, with its slanting chimney-smoke,
And close beside its porch a sleeping child,
His dear head pillowed on a sleeping dog—
One arm between its fore-legs, and the hand
Holds loosely its small handful of wild-flowers

Unfilletted, and of unequal lengths.
A curious picture, with a master's haste
Sketched on a strip of pinky-silver skin,   160
Peeled from the birchen bark! Divinest maid!
Yon bark her canvas, and those purple berries
Her pencil! See, the juice is scarcely dried
On the fine skin! She has been newly here;
And lo! yon patch of heath has been her couch—
The pressure still remains! O blesséd couch!
For this may'st thou flower early, and the sun,
Slanting at eve, rest bright, and linger long
Upon thy purple bells! O Isabel!
Daughter of genius! stateliest of our maids!   170
More beautiful than whom Alcaeus wooed,
The Lesbian woman of immortal song!
O child of genius! stately, beautiful,
And full of love to all, save only me,
And not ungentle e'en to me! My heart,
Why beats it thus? Through yonder coppice-wood
Needs must the pathway turn, that leads straightway
On to her father's house. She is alone!
The night draws on—such ways are hard to hit—
And fit it is I should restore this sketch,   180
Dropt unawares, no doubt. Why should I yearn
To keep the relique? 'twill but idly feed
The passion that consumes me. Let me haste!
The picture in my hand which she has left;
She cannot blame me that I followed her:
And I may be her guide the long wood through.

Hymn before Sun-Rise, in the Vale of Chamouni

Besides the Rivers, Arve and Arveiron, which have their sources in the foot of Mont Blanc, five conspicuous torrents rush down its sides; and within a few paces of the Glaciers, the Gentiana Major grows in immense numbers, with its "flowers of loveliest blue."

Hast thou a charm to stay the morning-star *
In his steep course? So long he seems to pause
On thy bald awful head, O sovran BLANC,
The Arve and Arveiron at thy base
Rave ceaselessly; but thou, most awful Form!
Risest from forth thy silent sea of pines,
How silently! Around thee and above
Deep is the air and dark, substantial, black,
An ebon mass: methinks thou piercest it,
As with a wedge! But when I look again,   10
It is thine own calm home, thy crystal shrine,
Thy habitation from eternity!
O dread and silent Mount! I gazed upon thee,
Till thou, still present to the bodily sense,
Didst vanish from my thought: entranced in prayer
I worshipped the Invisible alone.

Yet, like some sweet beguiling melody,
So sweet, we know not we are listening to it,
Thou, the meanwhile, wast blending with my Thought,
Yea, with my Life and Life's own secret joy: 20
Till the dilating Soul, enrapt, transfused,
Into the mighty vision passing—there
As in her natural form, swelled vast to Heaven!

Awake, my soul! not only passive praise
Thou owest! not alone these swelling tears,
Mute thanks and secret ecstasy! Awake,
Voice of sweet song! Awake, my heart, awake!
Green vales and icy cliffs, all join my Hymn.

Thou first and chief, sole sovereign of the Vale!
O struggling with the darkness all the night,   30
And visited all night by troops of stars,
Or when they climb the sky or when they sink:
Companion of the morning-star at dawn,
Thyself Earth's rosy star, and of the dawn
Co-herald: wake, O wake, and utter praise!
Who sank thy sunless pillars deep in Earth?

Who filled thy countenance with rosy light?
Who made thee parent of perpetual streams?

And you, ye five wild torrents fiercely glad!
Who called you forth from night and utter death,   40
From dark and icy caverns called you forth,
Down those precipitous, black, jaggéd rocks,
For ever shattered and the same for ever?
Who gave you your invulnerable life,
Your strength, your speed, your fury, and your joy,
Unceasing thunder and eternal foam?
And who commanded (and the silence came),
Here let the billows stiffen, and have rest?

Ye Ice-falls! ye that from the mountain's brow
Adown enormous ravines slope amain—   50
Torrents, methinks, that heard a mighty voice,
And stopped at once amid their maddest plunge!
Motionless torrents! silent cataracts!
Who made you glorious as the Gates of Heaven
Beneath the keen full moon? Who bade the sun
Clothe you with rainbows? Who, with living flowers
Of loveliest blue, spread garlands at your feet?—
GOD! let the torrents, like a shout of nations,
Answer! and let the ice-plains echo, GOD!
GOD! sing ye meadow-streams with gladsome voice!   60
Ye pine-groves, with your soft and soul-like sounds!
And they too have a voice, yon piles of snow,
And in their perilous fall shall thunder, GOD!

Ye living flowers that skirt the eternal frost!
Ye wild goats sporting round the eagle's nest!
Ye eagles, play-mates of the mountain-storm!
Ye lightnings, the dread arrows of the clouds!
Ye signs and wonders of the element!
Utter forth God, and fill the hills with praise!

Thou too, hoar Mount! with thy sky-pointing peaks,   70
Oft from whose feet the avalanche, unheard,

Shoots downward, glittering through the pure serene
Into the depth of clouds, that veil thy breast—
Thou too again, stupendous Mountain! thou
That as I raise my head, awhile bowed low
In adoration, upward from thy base
Slow travelling with dim eyes suffused with tears,
Solemnly seemest, like a vapoury cloud,
To rise before me—Rise, O ever rise,
Rise like a cloud of incense from the Earth!   80
Thou kingly Spirit throned among the hills,
Thou dread ambassador from Earth to Heaven,
Great Hierarch! tell thou the silent sky,
And tell the stars, and tell yon rising sun
Earth, with her thousand voices, praises GOD.

Inscription for a
Fountain on a Heath

This Sycamore, oft musical with bees,—
Such tents the Patriarchs loved! O long unharmed
May all its agéd boughs o'er-canopy
The small round basin, which this jutting stone
Keeps pure from falling leaves! Long may the Spring,
Quietly as a sleeping infant's breath,
Send up cold waters to the traveller
With soft and even pulse! Nor ever cease
Yon tiny cone of sand its soundless dance,
Which at the bottom, like a Fairy's Page,   10
As merry and no taller, dances still,
Nor wrinkles the smooth surface of the Fount.
Here Twilight is and Coolness: here is moss,
A soft seat, and a deep and ample shade.
Thou may'st toil far and find no second tree.
Drink, Pilgrim, here; Here rest! and if thy heart
Be innocent, here too shalt thou refresh
Thy spirit, listening to some gentle sound,
Or passing gale or hum of murmuring bees!

The Pains of Sleep

Ere on my bed my limbs I lay,
It hath not been my use to pray
With moving lips or bended knees;
But silently, by slow degrees,
My spirit I to Love compose,
In humble trust mine eye-lids close,
With reverential resignation,
No wish conceived, no thought exprest,
Only a sense of supplication;
A sense o'er all my soul imprest   10
That I am weak, yet not unblest,
Since in me, round me, every where
Eternal Strength and Wisdom are.

But yester-night I prayed aloud
In anguish and in agony,
Up-starting from the fiendish crowd
Of shapes and thoughts that tortured me:
A lurid light, a trampling throng,
Sense of intolerable wrong,
And whom I scorned, those only strong!   20
Thirst of revenge, the powerless will
Still baffled, and yet burning still!
Desire with loathing strangely mixed
On wild or hateful objects fixed.
Fantastic passions! maddening brawl!
And shame and terror over all!
Deeds to be hid which were not hid,
Which all confused I could not know
Whether I suffered, or I did:
For all seemed guilt, remorse or woe,   30
My own or others still the same
Life-stifling fear, soul-stifling shame.

So two nights passed: the night's dismay
Saddened and stunned the coming day.

Sleep, the wide blessing, seemed to me
Distemper's worst calamity.
The third night, when my own loud scream
Had waked me from the fiendish dream,
O'ercome with sufferings strange and wild,
I wept as I had been a child;   40
And having thus by tears subdued
My anguish to a milder mood,
Such punishments, I said, were due
To natures deepliest stained with sin,—
For aye entempesting anew
The unfathomable hell within,
The horror of their deeds to view,
To know and loathe, yet wish and do!
Such griefs with such men well agree,
But wherefore, wherefore fall on me?   50
To be beloved is all I need,
And whom I love, I love indeed.

Fragment: The Night-Mare Death in Life

I know 'tis but a dream, yet feel more anguish
Than if 'twere truth. It has been often so:
Must I die under it? Is no one near?
Will no one hear these stifled groans and wake me?

Phantom

All look and likeness caught from earth
All accident of kin and birth,
Had pass'd away. There was no trace
Of aught on that illumined face,
Uprais'd beneath the rifted stone
But of one spirit all her own;—
She, she herself, and only she,
Shone through her body visibly.

A Sunset

Upon the mountain's edge with light touch resting,
There a brief while the globe of splendour sits
   And seems a creature of the earth; but soon
      More changeful than the Moon,
To wane fantastic his great orb submits,
Or cone or mow of fire: till sinking slowly
Even to a star at length he lessens wholly.

Abrupt, as Spirits vanish, he is sunk!
A soul-like breeze possesses all the wood.
   The boughs, the sprays have stood   10
As motionless as stands the ancient trunk!
But every leaf through all the forest flutters,
And deep the cavern of the fountain mutters.

Metrical Feet

LESSON FOR A BOY

Trōchĕe trīps frŏm lōng tŏ shŏrt;
From long to long in solemn sort
Slōw Spōndēe stālks; strŏng fōot! yet ill able
Ĕvĕr tŏ cōme ŭp wĭth Dāctyl trĭsȳllăblĕ.
Iāmbĭcs mārch frŏm shŏrt tŏ lōng;—
Wĭth ă lēap ănd ă bōund thĕ swĭft Ānăpăests thrōng;
One syllable long, with one short at each side,
Ămphībrăchŷs hāstes wĭth ă stātelŷ stride;—
Fīrst ănd lāst bēĭng lōng, mĭddlĕ shŏrt, Ămphĭmācer
Strīkes hĭs thūndērĭng hōofs lĭke ă prōud
    hĭgh-brĕd Rācer.   10
If Derwent be innocent, steady, and wise,
And delight in the things of earth, water, and skies;
Tender warmth at his heart, with these metres to show it,
With sound sense in his brains, may make Derwent a
   poet,—
May crown him with fame, and must win him the love 15

Of his father on earth and his Father above.
        My dear, dear child!
Could you stand upon Skiddaw, you would not from its
    whole ridge
See a man who so loves you as your
    fond S. T. COLERIDGE.

To William Wordsworth

COMPOSED ON THE NIGHT AFTER HIS RECITATION OF A
POEM ON THE GROWTH OF AN INDIVIDUAL MIND *

Friend of the wise! and Teacher of the Good!
Into my heart have I received that Lay
More than historic, that prophetic Lay
Wherein (high theme by thee first sung aright)
Of the foundations and the building up
Of a Human Spirit thou hast dared to tell
What may be told, to the understanding mind
Revealable; and what within the mind
By vital breathings secret as the soul
Of vernal growth, oft quickens in the heart   10
Thoughts all too deep for words!—

                        Theme hard as high!
Of smiles spontaneous, and mysterious fears
(The first-born they of Reason and twin-birth),
Of tides obedient to external force,
And currents self-determined, as might seem,
Or by some inner Power; of moments awful,
Now in thy inner life, and now abroad,
When power streamed from thee, and thy soul received
The light reflected, as a light bestowed—
Of fancies fair, and milder hours of youth,   20
Hyblean murmurs of poetic thought *
Industrious in its joy, in vales and glens
Native or outland, lakes and famous hills!
Or on the lonely high-road, when the stars
Were rising; or by secret mountain-streams,

The guides and the companions of thy way!

Of more than Fancy, of the Social Sense
Distending wide, and man beloved as man,
Where France in all her towns lay vibrating
Like some becalméd bark beneath the burst   30
Of Heaven's immediate thunder, when no cloud
Is visible, or shadow on the main.
For thou wert there, thine own brows garlanded,
Amid the tremor of a realm aglow,
Amid a mighty nation jubilant,
When from the general heart of human kind
Hope sprang forth like a full-born Deity!
——Of that dear Hope afflicted and struck down,
So summoned homeward, thenceforth calm and sure
From the dread watch-tower of man's absolute self,   40
With light unwaning on her eyes, to look
Far on—herself a glory to behold,
The Angel of the vision! Then (last strain)
Of Duty, chosen Laws controlling choice,
Action and joy!—An Orphic song indeed,*
A song divine of high and passionate thoughts
To their own music chaunted!

                         O great Bard!
Ere yet that last strain dying awed the air,
With stedfast eye I viewed thee in the choir
Of ever-enduring men. The truly great   50
Have all one age, and from one visible space
Shed influence! They, both in power and act,
Are permanent, and Time is not with them,
Save as it worketh for them, they in it.
Nor less a sacred Roll, than those of old,
And to be placed, as they, with gradual fame
Among the archives of mankind, thy work
Makes audible a linkéd lay of Truth,
Of Truth profound a sweet continuous lay,
Not learnt, but native, her own natural notes!   60
Ah! as I listened with a heart forlorn,

The pulses of my being beat anew:
And even as Life returns upon the drowned,
Life's joy rekindling roused a throng of pains—
Keen pangs of Love, awakening as a babe
Turbulent, with an outcry in the heart;
And fears self-willed, that shunned the eye of Hope;
And Hope that scarce would know itself from Fear;
Sense of past Youth, and Manhood come in vain,
And Genius given, and Knowledge won in vain;   70
And all which I had culled in wood-walks wild,
And all which patient toil had reared, and all,
Commune with thee had opened out—but flowers
Strewed on my corse, and borne upon my bier
In the same coffin, for the self-same grave!

    That way no more! and ill beseems it me,
Who came a welcomer in herald's guise,
Singing of Glory, and Futurity,
To wander back on such unhealthful road,
Plucking the poisons of self-harm! And ill   80
Such intertwine beseems triumphal wreaths
Strew'd before thy advancing!

                              Nor do thou,
Sage Bard! impair the memory of that hour
Of thy communion with my nobler mind
By pity or grief, already felt too long!
Nor let my words import more blame than needs.
The tumult rose and ceased: for Peace is nigh
Where Wisdom's voice has found a listening heart.
Amid the howl of more than wintry storms,
The Halcyon hears the voice of vernal hours   90
Already on the wing.

                    Eve following eve,
Dear tranquil time, when the sweet sense of Home
Is sweetest! moments for their own sake hailed
And more desired, more precious, for thy song,
In silence listening, like a devout child,

                    [To William Wordsworth]   134

My soul lay passive, by thy various strain
Driven as in surges now beneath the stars,
With momentary stars of my own birth,
Fair constellated foam, still darting off
Into the darkness; now a tranquil sea,   100
Outspread and bright, yet swelling to the moon.

And when—O Friend! my comforter and guide!
Strong in thyself, and powerful to give strength!—
Thy long sustainéd Song finally closed,
And thy deep voice had ceased—yet thou thyself
Wert still before my eyes, and round us both
That happy vision of belovéd faces—
Scarce conscious, and yet conscious of its close
I sate, my being blended in one thought
(Thought was it? or aspiration? or resolve?)   110
Absorbed, yet hanging still upon the sound—
And when I rose, I found myself in prayer.

Recollections of Love

I

How warm this woodland wild Recess!
   Love surely hath been breathing here;
   And this sweet bed of heath, my dear!
Swells up, then sinks with faint caress,
   As if to have you yet more near.

II

Eight springs have flown, since last I lay
   On sea-ward Quantock's heathy hills,
   Where quiet sounds from hidden rills
Float here and there, like things astray,
   And high o'er head the sky-lark shrills.   10

III

No voice as yet had made the air
   Be music with your name; yet why

That asking look? that yearning sigh?
That sense of promise every where?
  Belovéd! flew your spirit by?

IV

As when a mother doth explore
  The rose-mark on her long-lost child,
  I met, I loved you, maiden mild!
As whom I long had loved before—
  So deeply had I been beguiled.   20

V

You stood before me like a thought,
  A dream remembered in a dream.
  But when those meek eyes first did seem
To tell me, Love within you wrought—
  O Greta, dear domestic stream!

VI

Has not, since then, Love's prompture deep,
  Has not Love's whisper evermore
  Been ceaseless, as thy gentle roar?
Sole voice, when other voices sleep,
  Dear under-song in clamor's hour.   30

To Two Sisters

[MARY MORGAN AND CHARLOTTE BRENT]

A WANDERER'S FAREWELL

To know, to esteem, to love,—and then to part—
Makes up life's tale to many a feeling heart;
Alas for some abiding-place of love,
O'er which my spirit, like the mother dove,
Might brood with warming wings!
                          O fair! O kind!
Sisters in blood, yet each with each intwined

More close by sisterhood of heart and mind!
Me disinherited in form and face
By nature, and mishap of outward grace;
Who, soul and body, through one guiltless fault   10
Waste daily with the poison of sad thought,
Me did you soothe, when solace hoped I none!
And as on unthaw'd ice the winter sun,
Though stern the frost, though brief the genial day,
You bless my heart with many a cheerful ray;
For gratitude suspends the heart's despair,
Reflecting bright though cold your image there.
Nay more! its music by some sweeter strain
Makes us live o'er our happiest hours again,
Hope re-appearing dim in memory's guise—   20
Even thus did you call up before mine eyes
Two dear, dear Sisters, prized all price above,
Sisters, like you, with more than sister's love;
So like you *they,* and so in *you* were seen
Their relative statures, tempers, looks, and mien,
That oft, dear ladies! you have been to me
At once a vision and reality.
Sight seem'd a sort of memory, and amaze
Mingled a trouble with affection's gaze.

Oft to my eager soul I whisper blame,   30
A Stranger bid it feel the Stranger's shame—
My eager soul, impatient of the name,
No strangeness owns, no Stranger's form descries:
The chidden heart spreads trembling on the eyes.
First-seen I gazed, as I would look you thro'!
My best-beloved regain'd their youth in you,—
And still I ask, though now familiar grown,
Are you for *their* sakes dear, or for your own?
O doubly dear! may Quiet with you dwell!

In Grief I love you, yet I love you well!   40
Hope long is dead to me! an orphan's tear
Love wept despairing o'er his nurse's bier.

[*To Two Sisters*] 137

Yet still she flutters o'er her grave's green slope:
For Love's despair is but the ghost of Hope!

Sweet Sisters! were you placed around one hearth
With those, your other selves in shape and worth,
Far rather would I sit in solitude,
Fond recollections all my fond heart's food,
And dream of *you*, sweet Sisters! (ah! not mine!)
And only *dream* of you (ah! dream and pine!)   50
Than boast the presence and partake the pride,
And shine in the eye, of all the world beside.

Psyche

The butterfly the ancient Grecians made *
The soul's fair emblem, and its only name—
But of the soul, escaped the slavish trade
Of mortal life!—For in this earthly frame
Ours is the reptile's lot, much toil, much blame,
Manifold motions making little speed,
And to deform and kill the things whereon we feed.

A Tombless Epitaph

'Tis true, Idoloclastes Satyrane! *
(So call him, for so mingling blame with praise,
And smiles with anxious looks, his earliest friends,
Masking his birth-name, wont to character
His wild-wood fancy and impetuous zeal,)
'Tis true that, passionate for ancient truths,
And honouring with religious love the Great
Of elder times, he hated to excess,
With an unquiet and intolerant scorn,
The hollow Puppets of a hollow Age,   10
Ever idolatrous, and changing ever
Its worthless Idols! Learning, Power, and Time,
(Too much of all) thus wasting in vain war

Of fervid colloquy. Sickness, 'tis true,
Whole years of weary days, besieged him close,
Even to the gates and inlets of his life!
But it is true, no less, that strenuous, firm,
And with a natural gladness, he maintained
The citadel unconquered, and in joy
Was strong to follow the delightful Muse.   20
For not a hidden path, that to the shades
Of the beloved Parnassian forest leads,
Lurked undiscovered by him; not a rill
There issues from the fount of Hippocrene,
But he had traced it upward to its source,
Through open glade, dark glen, and secret dell,
Knew the gay wild flowers on its banks, and culled
Its med'cinable herbs. Yea, oft alone,
Piercing the long-neglected holy cave,
The haunt obscure of old Philosophy,   30
He bade with lifted torch its starry walls
Sparkle, as erst they sparkled to the flame
Of odorous lamps tended by Saint and Sage.
O framed for calmer times and nobler hearts!
O studious Poet, eloquent for truth!
Philosopher! contemning wealth and death,
Yet docile, childlike, full of Life and Love!
Here, rather than on monumental stone,
This record of thy worth thy Friend inscribes,
Thoughtful, with quiet tears upon his cheek.   40

Time, Real and Imaginary

AN ALLEGORY

On the wide level of a mountain's head,*
(I knew not where, but 'twas some faery place)
Their pinions, ostrich-like, for sails out-spread,
Two lovely children run an endless race,
        A sister and a brother!
    This far outstripp'd the other;
Yet ever runs she with reverted face,

And looks and listens for the boy behind:
    For he, alas! is blind!
O'er rough and smooth with even step he passed,   10
And knows not whether he be first or last.

An Invocation

FROM *Remorse*

[Act III, Scene i, ll. 69-82.]

Hear, sweet Spirit, hear the spell,
Lest a blacker charm compel!
So shall the midnight breezes swell
With thy deep long-lingering knell.

And at evening evermore,
In a chapel on the shore,
Shall the chaunter, sad and saintly,
Yellow tapers burning faintly,
Doleful masses chaunt for thee,
    Miserere Domine!   10

Hush! the cadence dies away
  On the quiet moonlight sea:
The boatmen rest their oars and say,
    Miserere Domine!

Song

FROM *Zapolya*

A sunny shaft did I behold,
  From sky to earth it slanted:
And poised therein a bird so bold—
  Sweet bird, thou wert enchanted!

He sank, he rose, he twinkled, he trolled
  Within that shaft of sunny mist;

His eyes of fire, his beak of gold,
    All else of amethyst!

And thus he sang: "Adieu! adieu!
Love's dreams prove seldom true.   10
The blossoms they make no delay:
The sparkling dew-drops will not stay.
    Sweet month of May,
        We must away;
            Far, far away!
                To-day! to-day!"

Hunting Song

FROM *Zapolya*

Up, up! ye dames, and lasses gay!
To the meadows trip away.
'Tis you must tend the flocks this morn,
And scare the small birds from the corn.
    Not a soul at home may stay:
        For the shepherds must go
        With lance and bow
    To hunt the wolf in the woods to-day.

Leave the hearth and leave the house
To the cricket and the mouse: 10
Find grannam out a sunny seat,
With babe and lambkin at her feet.
    Not a soul at home may stay:
        For the shepherds must go
        With lance and bow
    To hunt the wolf in the woods to-day.

To Nature

It may indeed be phantasy, when I
    Essay to draw from all created things

Deep, heartfelt, inward joy that closely clings;
And trace in leaves and flowers that round me lie
Lessons of love and earnest piety.
    So let it be; and if the wide world rings
    In mock of this belief, it brings
Nor fear, nor grief, nor vain perplexity.
So will I build my altar in the fields,
    And the blue sky my fretted dome shall be,   10
And the sweet fragrance that the wild flower yields
    Shall be the incense I will yield to Thee,
Thee only God! and thou shalt not despise
Even me, the priest of this poor sacrifice.

Limbo

          *   *   *   *   *

The sole true Something—This! In Limbo's Den
It frightens Ghosts, as here Ghosts frighten men.
Thence cross'd unseiz'd—and shall some fated hour
Be pulveris'd by Demogorgon's power,*
And given as poison to annihilate souls—
Even now it shrinks them—they shrink in as Moles
(Nature's mute monks, live mandrakes of the ground)
Creep back from Light—then listen for its sound;—
See but to dread, and dread they know not why—
The natural alien of their negative eye.   10

'Tis a strange place, this Limbo!—not a Place,
Yet name it so;—where Time and weary Space
Fettered from flight, with night-mare sense of fleeing,
Strive for their last crepuscular half-being;—
Lank Space, and scytheless Time with branny hands
Barren and soundless as the measuring sands,
Not mark'd by flit of Shades,—unmeaning they
As moonlight on the dial of the day!
But that is lovely—looks like Human Time,—
An Old Man with a steady look sublime,   20
That stops his earthly task to watch the skies;

But he is blind—a Statue hath such eyes;—
Yet having moonward turn'd his face by chance,
Gazes the orb with moon-like countenance,
With scant white hairs, with foretop bald and high,
He gazes still,—his eyeless face all eye;—
As 'twere an organ full of silent sight,
His whole face seemeth to rejoice in light!
Lip touching lip, all moveless, bust and limb—
He seems to gaze at that which seems to gaze on him! 30
   No such sweet sights doth Limbo den immure,
Wall'd round, and made a spirit-jail secure,
By the mere horror of blank Naught-at-all,
Whose circumambience doth these ghosts enthral.
A lurid thought is growthless, dull Privation,
Yet that is but a Purgatory curse;
Hell knows a fear far worse,
A fear—a future state;—'tis positive Negation!

The Knight's Tomb

Where is the grave of Sir Arthur O'Kellyn?
Where may the grave of that good man be?—
By the side of a spring, on the breast of Helvellyn,
Under the twigs of a young birch tree!
The oak that in summer was sweet to hear,
And rustled its leaves in the fall of the year,
And whistled and roared in the winter alone,
Is gone,—and the birch in its stead is grown.—
The Knight's bones are dust,
And his good sword rust;—   10
His soul is with the saints, I trust.

On Donne's Poetry

With Donne, whose muse on dromedary trots,
Wreathe iron pokers into true-love knots;

Rhyme's sturdy cripple, fancy's maze and clue,
Wit's forge and fire-blast, meaning's press and screw.

Fragment

Truth I pursued, as Fancy sketch'd the way,
And wiser men than I went worse astray.

Youth and Age

Verse, a breeze mid blossoms straying,
Where Hope clung feeding, like a bee—
Both were mine! Life went a-maying
    With Nature, Hope, and Poesy,
        When I was young!

When I was young?—Ah, woful When!
Ah! for the change 'twixt Now and Then!
This breathing house not built with hands,
This body that does me grievous wrong,
O'er aery cliffs and glittering sands,
How lightly then it flashed along: —   10
Like those trim skiffs, unknown of yore,
On winding lakes and river wide,
That ask no aid of sail or oar,
That fear no spite of wind or tide!
Nought cared this body for wind or weather
When Youth and I lived in't together.

Flowers are lovely; Love is flower-like;
Friendship is a sheltering tree;
O! the joys, that came down shower-like,
Of Friendship, Love, and Liberty,
        Ere I was old!   20

Ere I was old? Ah woful Ere,
Which tells me, Youth's no longer here!

O Youth! for years so many and sweet,
'Tis known, that Thou and I were one,
I'll think it but a fond conceit—
It cannot be that Thou art gone!
Thy vesper-bell hath not yet toll'd:—
And thou wert aye a masker bold!
What strange disguise hast now put on,
To make believe, that thou art gone?   30
I see these locks in silvery slips,
This drooping gait, this altered size:
But Spring-tide blossoms on thy lips,
And tears take sunshine from thine eyes!
Life is but thought: so think I will
That Youth and I are house-mates still.

Dew-drops are the gems of morning,
But the tears of mournful eve!
Where no hope is, life's a warning
That only serves to make us grieve,
           When we are old: 40

That only serves to make us grieve
With oft and tedious taking-leave,
Like some poor nigh-related guest,
That may not rudely be dismist;
Yet hath outstay'd his welcome while,
And tells the jest without the smile.

Work without Hope

LINES COMPOSED 21ST FEBRUARY 1825

All Nature seems at work. Slugs leave their lair—
The bees are stirring—birds are on the wing—
And Winter slumbering in the open air,
Wears on his smiling face a dream of Spring!
And I the while, the sole unbusy thing,
Nor honey make, nor pair, nor build, nor sing.

Yet well I ken the banks where amaranths blow,*
Have traced the fount whence streams of nectar flow.
Bloom, O ye amaranths! bloom for whom ye may,
For me ye bloom not! Glide, rich streams, away!   10
With lips unbrightened, wreathless brow, I stroll:
And would you learn the spells that drowse my soul?
Work without Hope draws nectar in a sieve,
And Hope without an object cannot live.

Song

Though veiled in spires of myrtle-wreath,
Love is a sword which cuts its sheath,
And through the clefts itself has made,
We spy the flashes of the blade!

But through the clefts itself has made
We likewise see Love's flashing blade,
By rust consùmed, or snapt in twain;
And only hilt and stump remain.

Constancy to an Ideal Object

Since all that beat about in Nature's range,
Or veer or vanish; why should'st thou remain
The only constant in a world of change,
O yearning Thought! that liv'st but in the brain?
Call to the Hours, that in the distance play,
The faery people of the future day——
Fond Thought! not one of all that shining swarm
Will breathe on thee with life-enkindling breath,
Till when, like strangers shelt'ring from a storm,
Hope and Despair meet in the porch of Death!   10
Yet still thou haunt'st me; and though well I see,
She is not thou, and only thou art she,
Still, still as though some dear embodied Good,

[*Constancy to an Ideal Object*] 146

Some living Love before my eyes there stood
With answering look a ready ear to lend,
I mourn to thee and say—"Ah! loveliest friend!
That this the meed of all my toils might be,
To have a home, an English home, and thee!"
Vain repetition! Home and Thou are one.
The peacefull'st cot, the moon shall shine upon,   20
Lulled by the thrush and wakened by the lark,
Without thee were but a becalméd bark,
Whose Helmsman on an ocean waste and wide
Sits mute and pale his mouldering helm beside.

And art thou nothing? Such thou art, as when
The woodman winding westward up the glen
At wintry dawn, where o'er the sheep-track's maze
The viewless snow-mist weaves a glist'ning haze,
Sees full before him, gliding without tread,
An image with a glory round its head;*   30
The enamoured rustic worships its fair hues,
Nor knows he makes the shadow, he pursues!

Lines

SUGGESTED BY THE LAST WORDS OF BERENGARIUS
OB. ANNO DOM. 1088 *

No more 'twixt conscience staggering and the Pope
Soon shall I now before my God appear,
By him to be acquitted, as I hope;
By him to be condemnéd, as I fear.—

REFLECTION ON THE ABOVE

Lynx amid moles! had I stood by thy bed,
Be of good cheer, meek soul! I would have said:
I see a hope spring from that humble fear.
All are not strong alike through storms to steer
Right onward. What? though dread of threatened death

And dungeon torture made thy hand and breath   10
Inconstant to the truth within thy heart!
That truth, from which, through fear, thou twice didst
     start,
Fear haply told thee, was a learnéd strife,
Or not so vital as to claim thy life:
And myriads reached Heaven, who never knew
Where lay the difference 'twixt the false and true!

Ye, who secure 'mid trophies not your own,
Judge him who won them when he stood alone,
And proudly talk of recreant Berengare—   20
O first the age, and then the man compare!
That age how dark! congenial minds how rare!
No host of friends with kindred zeal did burn!
No throbbing hearts awaited his return!
Prostrate alike when prince and peasant fell,
He only disenchanted from the spell,
Like the weak worm that gems the starless night,
Moved in the scanty circlet of his light:
And was it strange if he withdrew the ray
That did but guide the night-birds to their prey?

The ascending day-star with a bolder eye   30
Hath lit each dew-drop on our trimmer lawn!
Yet not for this, if wise, shall we decry
The spots and struggles of the timid Dawn;
Lest so we tempt th' approaching Noon to scorn
The mists and painted vapours of our Morn.

Cologne

In Köhln, a town of monks and bones,
And pavements fang'd with murderous stones
And rags, and hags, and hideous wenches;
I counted two and seventy stenches,
All well defined, and several stinks!

Ye Nymphs that reign o'er sewers and sinks,
   The river Rhine, it is well known,
   Doth wash your city of Cologne;
But tell me, Nymphs, what power divine
Shall henceforth wash the river Rhine?   10

Phantom or Fact

A DIALOGUE IN VERSE

AUTHOR

A lovely form there sate beside my bed,
And such a feeding calm its presence shed,
A tender love so pure from earthly leaven,
That I unnethe the fancy might control,
'Twas my own spirit newly come from heaven,
Wooing its gentle way into my soul!
But ah! the change—it had not stirr'd, and yet—
Alas! that change how fain would I forget!
That shrinking back, like one that had mistook!
That weary, wandering, disavowing look!   10
'Twas all another, feature, look, and frame,
And still, methought, I knew, it was the same!

FRIEND

This riddling tale, to what does it belong?
Is't history? vision? or an idle song?
Or rather say at once, within what space
Of time this wild disastrous change took place?

AUTHOR

Call it a moment's work (and such it seems)
This tale's a fragment from the life of dreams;
But say, that years matur'd the silent strife,
And 'tis a record from the dream of life.   20

[Phantom or Fact]   149

Reason

["Finally, what is Reason? You have often asked me: and
this is my answer":—]

Whene'er the mist, that stands 'twixt God and thee,
Defecates to a pure transparency,
That intercepts no light and adds no stain—
There Reason is, and then begins her reign!

But alas!
    ——"tu stesso, ti fai grosso
  Col falso immaginar, sì che non vedi
  Ciò che vedresti, se l'avessi scosso." *

                    Dante, *Paradiso*, Canto i.

Self-Knowledge

    —E coelo descendit γνῶθι σεαυτόν—JUVENAL, xi. 27.

Γνῶθι σεαυτόν and is this the prime *
And heaven-sprung adage of the olden time!—
Say, canst thou make thyself?—Learn first that trade;—
Haply thou mayst know what thyself had made.
What hast thou, Man, that thou dar'st call thine own?—
What is there in thee, Man, that can be known?—
Dark fluxion, all unfixable by thought,
A phantom dim of past and future wrought,
Vain sister of the worm,—life, death, soul, clod—
Ignore thyself, and strive to know thy God!   10

Love's Apparition and Evanishment

AN ALLEGORIC ROMANCE

Like a lone Arab, old and blind,
Some caravan had left behind,
Who sits beside a ruin'd well,
Where the shy sand-asps bask and swell;
And now he hangs his agéd head aslant,
And listens for a human sound—in vain!
And now the aid, which Heaven alone can grant,
Upturns his eyeless face from Heaven to gain;—
Even thus, in vacant mood, one sultry hour,
Resting my eye upon a drooping plant,   10
With brow low-bent, within my garden-bower,
I sate upon the couch of camomile;
And—whether 'twas a transient sleep, perchance,
Flitted across the idle brain, the while
I watch'd the sickly calm with aimless scope,
In my own heart; or that, indeed a trance,
Turn'd my eye inward—thee, O genial Hope,
Love's elder sister! thee did I behold,
Drest as a bridesmaid, but all pale and cold,
With roseless cheek, all pale and cold and dim,   20
   Lie lifeless at my feet!
And then came Love, a sylph in bridal trim,
   And stood beside my seat;
She bent, and kiss'd her sister's lips,
   As she was wont to do;—
Alas! 'twas but a chilling breath
Woke just enough of life in death
   To make Hope die anew.

L'ENVOY

In vain we supplicate the Powers above;
There is no resurrection for the Love   30
That, nursed in tenderest care, yet fades away
In the chill'd heart by gradual self-decay.

Epitaph

Stop, Christian passer-by!—Stop, child of God,
And read with gentle breast. Beneath this sod
A poet lies, or that which once seem'd he.
O lift one thought in prayer for S. T. C.;
That he who many a year with toil of breath
Found death in life, may here find life in death!
Mercy for praise—to be forgiven for fame
He ask'd, and hoped, through Christ. Do thou the same!

Notes

William Lisle Bowles (1762–1850) was a minor poet of whom Coleridge said, "surely never was a writer so equal in excellence!" The first chapter of *Biographia Literaria* describes Coleridge's early enthusiasm for Bowles.

The Aeolian harp, named from Aeolus, god of the winds, is a stringed instrument which produces music when a current of air blows through it. The image is recurrent in Coleridge's poetry.

Lines 26-33, with their Wordsworthian affinities, were first included in the poem in 1828.

To line 60 Coleridge appended as a note a statement in French of Mme. Roland asserting that the atheist lacks, not reason, but a sense of feeling.

In 1817 Coleridge attached two lines to the end of the poem:

> We must not think so; but forget and forgive,
> And what Heaven gives life to, we'll still let it live.

He later commented on his addition: "Added thro' a cowardly fear of the Goody! What a Hollow where the Heart of Faith ought to be, does it not betray? this alarm concerning Christian morality, that will not permit even a Raven to be a Raven, nor a Fox a Fox, but demands conventicular justice to be inflicted on their unchristian conduct, or at least an antidote to be annexed."

THIS LIME-TREE BOWER

Motto: Ch. and Mary Lamb—dear to my heart, yea, as it were my Heart.—S.T.C. Aet. 63; 1834—1797–1834 37 years! [Marginal note written by Coleridge in an 1834 edition of his works.]

Line 17: The *Asplenium Scolopendrium,* called in some countries the Adder's Tongue, in others the Hart's Tongue. . . . [Coleridge's note.]

Line 76: Coleridge noted that by "creeking" he meant to describe the sound of birds' quill feathers working against each other in flight.

THE RIME OF THE ANCIENT MARINER

The motto, from the works of the seventeenth-century divine, Thomas Burnet, may be translated as follows: I readily believe that there are more invisible beings in the universe than visible. But who shall explain to us the nature, the rank and kinship, the distinguishing marks and graces of each? What do they do? Where do they dwell? The human mind has circled round this knowledge, but never attained to it. Yet there is profit, I do not doubt, in sometimes contemplating in the mind, as in a picture, the image of greater and better worlds: lest the intellect, habituated to the petty details of daily life, should be contracted within too narrow limits and settle down wholly on trifles. But, meanwhile, a watchful eye must be kept on truth, and proportion observed, that we may distinguish the certain from the uncertain, day from night.

Line 227: For the last two lines of this stanza, I am indebted to Mr. Wordsworth. It was on a delightful walk from Nether Stowey to Dulverton, with him and his sister, in the Autumn of 1797, that this Poem was planned, and in part composed. [Coleridge's note.]

Line 132: The evil spirit cannot cross the threshold under her own power, but must be helped by one who dwells within.

Line 350: *Pike:* peak.

Line 351: *Ghyll:* valley.

Line 365: *Plight:* most likely an archaic form of "plait."

Lines 408-426: Coleridge called these lines "the best and sweetest lines that I ever wrote." They may refer indirectly to the estrangement between Coleridge and Southey.

FROST AT MIDNIGHT

Line 15: In all parts of the kingdom these films are called *strangers* and supposed to portend the arrival of some absent friend. [Coleridge's note.]

FRANCE: AN ODE

In 1802 Coleridge added the following argument to his poem:

> *First Stanza.* An invocation to those objects in Nature the contemplation of which had inspired the Poet with a devotional love of Liberty. *Second Stanza.* The exultation of the poet at the commencement of the French Revolution, and his unqualified abhorrence of the Alliance against the Republic. *Third Stanza.* The blasphemies and horrors during the domination of the Terrorists regarded by the Poet as a transient storm, and as the natural consequence of the former despotism and of the foul superstition of Popery. Reason, indeed, began to suggest many apprehensions; yet still the Poet struggled to retain the hope that France would make conquests by no other means than by presenting to the observation of Europe a people more happy and better instructed than under other forms of Government. *Fourth Stanza.* Switzerland, and the Poet's recantation. *Fifth Stanza.*

An address to Liberty, in which the Poet expresses his conviction that those feelings and that grand *ideal* of Freedom which the mind attains by its contemplation of its individual nature, and of the sublime surrounding objects (see Stanza the First) do not belong to men, as a society, nor can possibly be either gratified or realised, under any form of human government; but belong to the individual man, so far as he is pure, and inflamed with the love and adoration of God in Nature.

Line 25: The poet describes his joy at the commencement of the French Revolution in 1789. In succeeding lines he describes his disapproval of England's membership in the European coalition, formed in 1793 after the execution of Louis XVI.

Line 43: There are a number of specific historical references in this stanza, first to the revolutionary government's renunciation of Christianity, then (lines 45-48) to the Reign of Terror, which began in 1792 and ended (see lines 49-50) in the winter of 1794.

Line 67: The French armies invaded Switzerland (Helvetia) early in 1798, shortly before this poem was published.

FEARS IN SOLITUDE

N.B. The above [poem] is perhaps not Poetry,—but rather a sort of middle thing between Poetry and Oratory—sermoni propriora.—Some parts are, I am conscious, too tame even for animated prose. [Coleridge's note.]

THE NIGHTINGALE

Line 13: The phrase quoted is Milton's description of the nightingale's song in "Il Penseroso" (line 62).

Line 39: Philomela, the poetic name for the nightingale, is derived from the myth of the queen who was changed by the gods into a nightingale as she fled from her sister's brutal husband, Tereus.

BALLAD OF THE DARK LADIÉ

When the poem, "Love" (see p. 113) was first published Coleridge called it, "Introduction to the Tale of the Dark Ladié."

HEXAMETERS

These "Hexameters" (a six foot dactylic line) were sent in a letter written in the winter of 1798–99 . . . to the Wordsworths. [E. H. Coleridge's note.]

LOVE

This poem, which may be supposed to refer to Coleridge's first meeting with Sara Hutchinson, was originally called, "Introduction to the Tale of the Dark Ladié." (See above.)

DEJECTION

The earliest version of this poem was sent in a letter of April, 1802, to Sara Hutchinson. It was she who was originally addressed in lines 25 and 47, though in later versions the poet changed the name to "William" (Wordsworth), "Edmund," and finally, "Lady."

Line 120: "Otway" was originally "William." The tale referred to in lines 118-125 is the story of Wordsworth's "Lucy Gray."

HYMN BEFORE SUN-RISE

The poem is a four-fold expansion of a translation of Friederika Brun's "Ode to Chamouny."

TO WILLIAM WORDSWORTH

Subtitle: The occasion is Wordsworth's reading from "The Prelude."

Line 21: *Hyblean:* honeyed.

Line 45: Orphic poetry (after Orpheus, the greatest poet and musician of classical myth) means poetry of mystic and prophetic power.

PSYCHE

In Greek Psyche is the common name for the soul and the butterfly. [Coleridge's note.]

A TOMBLESS EPITAPH

Sir Satyrane, "A Satyres son yborne in forrest wylde" (Spenser's *Faery Queene*, Book I, Canto vi), rescues Una from the violence of Sarazin. Coleridge may have regarded Satyrane as the anonym of Luther. [E. H. Coleridge's note.] Coleridge published some of his own letters from Germany under the title, *Satyrane's Letters*. Idoloclast, Coleridge himself explained, is a "breaker of idols."

TIME, REAL AND IMAGINARY

By imaginary Time, I meant the state of a school boy's mind when on his return to school he projects his being in his day dreams, and lives in his next holidays, six months hence; and this I contrasted with real Time. [Coleridge's note.]

LIMBO

Line 4: *Demogorgon:* a mysterious and terrifying infernal deity.

WORK WITHOUT HOPE

Line 7: Amaranth is not only a real flower, but in poetic tradition the flower that never fades.

CONSTANCY TO AN IDEAL OBJECT

Line 30: Coleridge noted that this was a phenomenon he had himself observed. A person's shadow, projected against mist, sometimes shows a glow around the head which gives it a spectral appearance.

LINES SUGGESTED BY THE LAST WORDS OF BERENGARIUS

Berengarius (or Berengar) of Tours (998–1088) was a celebrated scholar who asserted that man must avail himself of reason, and that when reason and authority conflict, reason must be followed. He came into conflict with official teaching on the doctrine of transubstantiation and, after being condemned by numerous councils, recanted his heretical beliefs.

REASON

The quotation (lines 88-90, Canto I, of the *Paradiso*) may be translated: "Thou, thyself, makest thyself dense with false imagining, and so thou seest not what thou wouldst see, if thou hadst cast it off."

SELF-KNOWLEDGE

The Greek phrase, announced from the heavens, is the motto carved over the portals of the Oracle at Delphi: "Know Thyself."

*contemplate the joys which
we cannot
share* (handwritten)

Other editions in the LAUREL POETRY SERIES